BEAUT
BARBARIANS

lesbian
feminist
poetry

edited by Lilian Mohin

radical feminist and lesbian publishers

Published in 1986 by Onlywomen Press,
radical feminist and lesbian publishers,
38 Mount Pleasant, London WC1X 0AP.

Cover illustration by Tristan Armstrong
Typeset by Columns of Reading
Printed and bound by Redwood Burn Ltd, Trowbridge,
Wiltshire

British Library Cataloguing in Publication Data

Beautiful Barbarians : Lesbian Feminist Poetry
  1. English poetry—Women authors
  2. English poetry—20th Century
  3. Lesbianism—Poetry
  I. Mohin, Lilian
  821'.914'08353   PR1177

ISBN 0-906500-23-0

CONTENTS

FOREWORD

This anthology was made possible by the political efforts and advances of the past 15–20 years. Lesbianism is central to feminism, the logical as well as emotional core of what will change the world. The very few other anthologies of lesbian poetry (or lesbian prose) have also stemmed from some variation upon this essentially political theme.

Reading lesbian literary criticism, lesbian history and lesbian feminist theory is reading about a series of discoveries, detective stories, the effort to unveil as much as create. We write without the context of a well established or widely known lesbian literary tradition or an acknowledged way of life. So, recent lesbian anthologies have tried to be inclusive, even representative.

Looking at these collections and reading the work of lesbian poets made it clear that this volume could be enormous, even if it contained only the work of already well known poets. I wanted, instead, to concentrate on the work of a few of us, choosing poems representative of each poet's concerns rather than representative of a movement or reflective of what has already been published. (The work in this anthology has not been published elsewhere in book form except in three instances.)

Onlywomen Press published Britain's first anthology of feminist poetry *One Foot on the Mountain*, at a time when the book felt as much a part of an active women's liberation movement as a literary artifact. The commonality of purpose (with concomitant fervour and enthusiasm) which characterised feminism in the '70s isn't evident in Britain in the '80s. Lesbians work toward significant change, develop skills and politics in what often feels like isolation. With this book, I hope to make more public (some of) the continuing growth of lesbian strengths and perceptions.

As I collected the work in this anthology, I was struck by what seems to me a new — for feminists — concern with form, with literary traditions. Several of the poets here flaunt the fun of playing with words. They work with established literary modes and mainstream conventions as well as with the more direct, everyday speech forms of radical feminist poetry. This attention to structure heightens the lucidity of lesbian feminist imagination and, of course, our enlightened inventiveness goes some way toward revitalising these forms.

Where and how we meet mainstream constrictions and expectations concerns all the poets here. Because of our position in (not of) a limited oppressive world we see that world especially clearly. But poets do more than report the view. While irony suffuses most lesbian work, and the poems in this collection are no exception, some of the poets here work explicitly on redefinition. Bonds with our biological families, either embraced or enforced, are scrutinised and reworked. Ethnic origins are reclaimed and then examined with a loving insistence on recognition — from lesbians on the one hand, from our reclaimed communities on the other. Other poets are more concerned with transformation. They clothe perception with fantasy, giving us entirely new worlds built upon inside knowledge of this one.

Terms like redefinition and transformation are abstract, accurate but not precise. The sixteen poets in BEAUTIFUL BARBARIANS* give them substance and moving reality. Read, enjoy, let us know what you think.

Lilian Mohin

*The title was taken from Suniti Namjoshi's poem, *A Consummation*, the final poem in this anthology.

ACKNOWLEDGEMENTS

Poems in this anthology which have been previously published elsewhere are listed below according to author.

Gillian Hanscombe: 'Hecate's Charm 4' and 'Hecate's Charm 8', *Hecate's Charms*, Kashmik Poets, Sydney, 1975 and Sappho, London, 1977.

Judith Barrington: 'Four Days in Spain', *Trying to be an Honest Woman*, Eighth Mountain Press, Oregon, 1985.

Marilyn Hacker: 'Corona' first appeared in *Massachusetts Review*. 'Grief and I want to take it up in you' and 'First, I want to make you come in my hand', *Love, Death and the Changing of the Seasons*, Arbor House, New York, 1986. 'Toward Autumn' *Assumptions*, Alfred A. Knopf, New York, 1985, 'Canzone' and 'Iva's Pantoum', *Taking Notice*, Alfred A. Knopf, New York, 1980.

Suniti Namjoshi: 'Tryptich' first appeared in *Canadian Literature*. 'Narrative Distance' first appeared in *Descant*.

Photographs appearing in this anthology are copyright each photographer as listed below according to subject.

Marg Yeo, Ruth Adam, Sheila Shulman, Joy Howard, Suniti Namjoshi and Gillian Hanscombe by Brenda Prince. Bernardine Evaristo by Mumtaz Karimjee. Jackie Kay by Ingrid Pollard. Andrea Loewenstein and Mary Dorcey by Mimsy Møller. Tina Kendall by Sarah Walton. Caroline Griffin by Sandra Hopley. Meg Kelly by Lottie Joseph. Marilyn Hacker by Irish Times. J.P. Hollerith by Koretz Studios. Judith Barrington by Ruth Gundle.

MARG YEO: i'm 40, have been employed variously as a secretary, antiquarian bookseller, clerk, computer operator, lecturer, and now as a literacy/numeracy tutor, but my real and, i hope, permanent work is writing [poems, an unwieldy novel and anything else that comes along]. and it's all because of women.

not so simple

i want to swallow you
whole   and reaching out to snag
you there you are in
me already   looking
smug and tentative stretched
out along a rib
                  your small fist has
hold of my whole heart.

this is not so
simple   one good
squeeze and i'd stutter down to
a dead stop
              i don't know you *that*
well   how can i
trust you in the very
beat and the breath of me?

"aren't you scared?" you
ask me sharp-eyed and i start to answer "yes
yes" but it's not there and
"no" i say with my heart in my
mouth and you still
hanging on to it

you look me over and it's
true [how could I hide
it from you hanging
onto my heart?]

                you
laugh and shift and
slither in drawing my
breath in after you down
deeper and deeper till i
am in my simple
hand holding onto your
heart

to say yes

to say
yes
the explosion of
leaf into
light

some
things grow
over the edges of
explanation
              and there is no
reading between
lines because there are no
longer any lines
and no more need for
reading

to find this so
sudden in each other
is to find ourselves with a

shock and instantaneous
sunk in an ocean bigger
than our puddle
bound comprehension can take
in   or swept up
into an air with no
horizons

there are no
coasts or foothills
here nothing to
climb nothing to
cling to or
hide behind

unless we choose
to be invisible not to be
known

        so much
easier to stay
strangers with
everything to say and
nothing to learn

than to say
yes

than to say
we have been
waiting all our lives
for this un
winding of rooftop and
rafter of the tough
fabric and fabrication

we put on
out of the womb

but we can
not be satisfied with
less

not satisfied
with a cold and singular
hole in the dumb
earth for
each of us

when we might un
tomb each
other with
a word
            bear
down   give
birth to a common
language

            say
yes

being canadian

i.
i'm doing it again   help
me
    (and you're saying "what? doing
what again?" thinking of
suicide of going
under giving
in)
      but it's not
that   i mean i'm
falling in love
again and being
canadian about it distant
and diffident

                [it must
be all those acres of snow empty
roads and the big
guns over the
border eyeing our
emptiness that make us
watch our
words

        we
are   i
am   always
afraid of the
invader plunking a heavy
kettle down on my
doorstep to coddle me into
tea or bubble my
bones up to a
lather and
wash me away]

and so i say
          "o are you
here again?" when i mean i've
missed you   and i push you
out of the car into dark dangerous streets and
drive away not looking
back   not
saying your
eyes your hair your
hands move in
me pound the
rock of my belly down to
sand that shifts and
drifts in the soft
beating of your
breath

ii.
this is the first
step towards
surrender
          i'm tip
toeing out of the frozen
north and stripping
down for summer
                    very
quietly of
course
      very
canadian

muttering under my
breath that perhaps i'll
go around
naked when you're
near un
armed venus with a big

welcoming crescent
of a smile to
embrace you in

can you come to
dinner?

bring your
kettle

move
in

rock bottom
[for sara and jenny]

i.
when i hit
rock
bottom i was
scared

it was so bloody
deep so
dark so edgeless
                  and so very
empty

     up quite
out of the
question unreachable and out of

sight if i had any
eyes to see

so it was just
me and the rock
bottom of things and the thick
thumb of absolutely
everything smeared me
flat on it

ii.
now you're sitting   tea cups half way
up to your lips   wanting to
know how i peeled
off got up
again into this
kitchen

          my dears it was so
simple

          there's me paper
dolling it under the
steamroller of my
life doing
myself down

               and
last but not
lightly i had to
laugh
          a rock
bottom belly
laugh

i
am the
belly into which i
fall

    i
am the
rock the
bottom
      and the
beginning of it all

dark of the moon   a letter to judi

i.
old friend   i've had a thin
night of it again walking with
helen who is twelve years dead and
laughs like the old days
                     i expect to forget
better than this   i expect
not to remember after this long the
textures gestures the angular
crook of an elbow as she draws me again out of a
crowd into a momentary clearing and
sets me down   shaping a landscape i can
catch my breath in
                (here is the pond   and over
there   on the far bank in the reeds and the
undergrowth   are the ducks
                  she calls them
and they come

          while around us
ten thousand people shift and eddy
away   afraid to get their feet wet)

ii.
old friend   we are still
choosing each other after this
long after the separations after the
years of living together
                    and this is not
what i expected
             each night this week
i've walked around our history got
drunk with david sat for hours at the kitchen
table with your mother talking
about you

       (i want to die
first   i could not bear to
miss you that much and
unremittingly)

           i want to use
big words that we are
synchronous congruent where we touch and even
at a distance
          but always you are
there with your arms out asking are we
all right am i
thinking about you

iii.
old friend i am
thinking about you even here in the

dark of the moon walking with
helen who is twelve years dead and dug
down deep in me laughs
like the old days

                    i am still
choosing you   and making it
solid

        (here is the pond   over
there on the far bank are the
ducks
            if we call they will still
swim to us

eating up everything
[for kay and barbara]

i.
reading aloud in the evening   high and
dry above the crash and tumble of upper
street behind a window box   over the bread
and the wine   spreading words like
butter   like soft cheese   our odd tri-partite eve
digs in
            picking the pieces of a poem
up from a littered
desk a littered life   and smoothing them
out between the salt and the sugar bowl

but not too smooth
                    this is stone
ground whole meal a rough
texture on the tongue a full belly

ii.
as a child i ate with
caution   picked over my plate kept my
marbles under my tongue   and didn't swallow much
of anything

                growing
up is only part of it
                        there is a sadness
gets in   you learn to live with it   but it dries
the bread in your mouth and
dulls the flavour   the taste is
metallic and middle-aged

the poems go
slow

iii
but fortnightly on fridays barbara slices the
mushrooms and recounts her week   kay mixes the
dressing and getting oiled up slips a word in
edgewise   i am setting the table
slicing the bread   and giving
thanks for the mercy of
choice in a thin life
                        when somebody pulls the
cork and pours
                and we're off again
to melbourne boston ottawa and
everywhere else there is   holding each

other laughing talking with our mouths
full (wishing our
mothers could see us now)   and eating up
everything

what i mean/by green

considerably more
jovial than a
frog on a frigid
lily-pad, in the winter
sun, i consider
the nature of
green:

you might
be inclined to think
i mean grass (in
any variety), or bread
mould
          but i am more
fruitful, meaning
that apple-green
spring sky you
thought was
blue, but birds
know as the un
imaginably palest fingers
of air, stroking green
thoughts thru an opening
wing   or the apple
bud hardly begun

stuffing its small
green exploding head head-
long out into apple
tree's greenest
breath, expiring
green
green
onto the long
smooth skin of summer

(so
warm, is what i mean
by green)

got the blues

got the
blues
blues
blues
behind the
eyes

not the momma
won't you please
come home kinda
blues, or even lost my
baby in a rainstorm
late
last tues
day night

but blue the warm
arms of mid
night so deep you
don't have any
eyes, folds you
up, soft, and a long
time gone
              or sharp blue
pain of grass, all
light and blade by
blade, stripping the naked
foot of summer
down to each bare
delicious bone
                while sun
slices blue heat in
to the thin
flesh, un
wrapping winter, and
plants the cleanest
blues
blues
blues
behind the
eyes

there are so many

you are making me an offer i can't
refuse   and you are
pleased about it   though the fact that i am drunk
   perhaps
slows your pleasure and you smile un
easy   look away when i laugh
                              and i can't help
laughing   though what kicks the laughter out
over my wine glass is not joy but
anger   grief   and a tearing love that
strips my skin off so i stand bare
naked to the bone   and
luminous with indignation.

there are so
few of us you say   offering me entry into the
elect   the gifted few   the politically
sound and technically delightful liberal polite left
wing and very pretty coterie of
poets
        there are so few
of us you say   not seeing the thin dark
haired woman leaning by the piano whom i have
loved for years   watching her pare
down to the bone till   as she leans now with her
arm round an old lover singing an old
song   the bareness of her beauty tears
at my eyes and there is a poem in this that she
or i or both
of us will write
                  not seeing
that it does not matter which
of us gets that down

                    not seeing that
one of us will
                    not seeing that you are the only
man in this room full of women whose hands are
   stained with
ink and bruised with beating at your
condescension   your patronage   your careful
distinguishing of art from everything
else
      not seeing that when i label
you in this way   there is no
escape from it   any more than i can
escape from being a woman and from having already
long ago chosen this difficult
saying where words are bare as
bone and belong to the body   each word a
rib a vertebra essential delicate and
common as women in the world

not seeing that we permit
each other this   and give
it   that a poem here is a bandage for a
wound   a shout of defiance   a quiet
woman taking her life in her hands and
passing it on

you have not looked at our
faces   what we have chosen
shows

        look at the dark haired woman
leaning by the piano   she wears a white
tee shirt and black trousers   she is surprisingly
thin and astoundingly
painfully beautiful   especially where the
bones show

                she
writes   she or
i could be writing this poem
                              (have you
guessed by now that i am
refusing your offer?)
                        she or i or any
one of these women could be
writing this poem

                    there are so
many of us

another love poem

i
women with sad
faces   mouths settling naturally
downward in repose   stretch more than half
naked and everywhere around me

unable to see myself   and knowing how i
squint against the sun   i try to imagine my
mouth curving naturally
upward   or at least neutral   an even thoughtful
line
      but as i do   lying here more than half
naked wearing my mother's body   my eyes fill
up   the tears pushing over and thundering
down to catch the corners of my
mouth   my mother's mouth   pulling them
down to make a riverbed
                          my face is a

waterfall
           my head some vast
cleft into a dangerous
underground where this out
pouring hurls itself up from some immensely deep
and dark and secret source in which my whole
life   each grief   each word   each slight and subtle
gesture   is caught   instant by instant   and left
hanging
           i am an
exhibition no one can see into except when that
pulse   that tide   rises and sweeps it
up and out and all over me

ii
it's sunday

over coffee nicolle
cries   then i cry   then we both
cry
    i don't know if anyone
notices
        we hold
hands while we remember

these days i see so many
tears
      not all for
grief   they seem to be sweeping us into our
forties and we're not even grown
up yet
        and still we know too
much   we have been every
where seen
everything
            we have no
illusions

iii
a life with no illusions can be a life
in which nothing at all takes
place
        or a life lived in a
war zone where every moment is potentially
explosive   where we go armed against the unexpected
    and
the expected and where we must
work together if we are to save
anything
we need to learn
not to make the same lethal mistakes
again
        stop
waiting for someone to sweep in and
save us knowing for sure that if the cavalry
arrived all sweat and jingling
spurs it would be our more than half
naked bodies they would
trample into the dirt and leave to lie out
under the sun

iv
she
sidestepped into my life   my friend tells
me   because she wanted to learn how to write
verse less badly   and
nothing else whatever she says now in
amazement

                that's not how it
happens   behind the blockades we are
starving   we have to
swallow each other whole and without asking
too many questions

                    we have to take everything
on faith [there is no
choice] we have to
trust each other   we cannot afford to be
divided against
ourselves   divided within
ourselves   any
longer

v
within ourselves against
ourselves

sometimes   we are our own worst
enemies
            every conversation   every
touch   sharpens up into edges and hard
words
        sometimes we use
each other   badly   and forget to say
love love love when it is most
required of us

[on the coach coming back from
edinburgh   we sat
silent and apart   as if there was
nothing to say
                    for two
years we sat silent and
apart
        except the night   you
drunk and i with a new
lover   you placed yourself   over and over   with
drunken
precision in my line of
sight   you were

waiting me out
                the most
stubborn woman in the world was
one (or both) of us]

vi
sometimes there can be nothing
other than my
hand in your
strong hand
                we didn't plan
it this way   we didn't even
guess where it might lead to   our
taking each other up like this on a
look and a promise

it was all
accident
        i wasn't looking and looked
up and there you were   in a
bookstore   across a crowd   at the back of a
meeting   alone in a
room   and i liked you or i
didn't   but you thought i was
interesting and you liked
me   or i made you
nervous or i made you
laugh till the tears poured down your
cheeks and i couldn't help laughing too
in spite of myself

so there we were trying to be
careful cautious
                    still testing the ground when we were
swept away and

plunged to a depth we weren't ready
for   with nothing to hold
to trust in but each
other

vii
more than half
naked   we've come a long way to end up
here   sweating in the
sun

    [just beyond
me   on the grass   a woman with a sad
face lifts her head and
hooks herself on my eyes
                              her eyes are
steady and
certain about all
sorts of things   she is
not in a hurry
                  we stare so long we are
complicit
            when her mouth twitches and turns
upward   i am implicated   i can't help but
follow her]

[this is another
love poem

JACKIE KAY: I was born in Edinburgh in 1961 and brought up in Glasgow. I've had poems published in *Artrage*, *Feminist Review* and various other magazines. Some of my poems are published in the *Angels of Fire Anthology* (Chatto and Windus). A collection of my poems was published by Sheba in *A Dangerous Knowing: Four Black Women Poets*.

I have short stories published in *Everyday Matters 2* by Sheba and another in *Stepping Out* by Pandora. My first play *Chiaroscuro* was presented by the Theatre of Black Women in 1986 and toured for three months. At the moment I'm working on another play for upper secondary school children on the theme of sexuality. I wrote the brief film script for BBC Split Screen series on *Pornography The Right to Choose*.

As a Black feminist I see writing as a political activity, one way to contribute to the struggle for change.

Witness

Nobody made any promises
that night when the moon slid
out of sight and the dark
could not begin to hold
our secret yet
somebody must have known
like the certainty
– the rain's going to come

I waited for you
whilst you methodically washed
every bit of your body

Maybe somebody heard
the howl – is it ghost that roam tonight
when that field was freshly dug
by nobody's hand
and piles of potatoes
sat like witnesses

I watched you
rise out of the bubbles
and wrap the towel around
and clean the bath

Later, the old woman
said she saw
but nobody believed she did
for the moon had left no light
and the street lamps all went out
refusing to witness

You rubbed cocoa butter
all over and said quietly
do you want to come through

Everybody must have slept
when the bats weren't sleeping
hanging upside down with
their eyes all open
bats don't do that

the old woman tried to say

and again nobody listened

Did you hear that
you jumped up
the bed tried to hold the shock
— and has somebody died?

Next morning
your face held its own secret
like a silent pride
and we looked out
on the street and all the magic
had gone with the morning coming
and the clock never insists
at night like now
clothes taken off slowly
hurried on and tea swallowed hot
and work calls not us crying out
for each other

daybreak broke passion
like splintered soft glass.

InterCity Through Spring

And I travel on an inter-city
through spring – the ground's lost
its ravaged winter look
wild flowers blow an offering
to the eye that stood still awhile
when winter – bold in bareness –
stretched itself across my vision
and now sped-fast into spring
the trees not yet full of green
nor blossom but the buds are
pushing determined to open out
this full sun afternoon

and she is with me
last night's passion spent
after all that season's waiting
it was spring that brought us forth
the loaded cry
our rhythm pumping blood
our sounds amplified beats
and this is for real   afterall
your warmth spreading my
old winter pains   out
your body carrying me through
to our season's offering
a risk   a burst
'let me take you there oh take you there'
we laugh remember the times
we held back in winter
pushing each other
thigh on high, take me I say take me there
and eager for bloom

and you know something?
that empty this winter's going to last forever feeling
has left me:
the pregnant waiting
broke its waters
and the   earth soaked up
every last drop.

Some Nights in Brooklyn and the Blood

I
I was pulled out with forceps
left a gash down my left cheek
and pus that took months
to dry up – I nearly died
four months inside a glass cot
not what I lost
but what I gained.

she came faithful
from Glasgow to Edinburgh
and peered through the glass
I must have felt somebody
wanting me to survive
against the odds
she would not 'pick another baby'

she brought me up
on cuddles and Campsie Glens
Burns suppers and wild mountain thyme
Glaswegian humour
and all the blooming heather
the moors empty as after
the bloody thing out of the womb
what roads I travelled to get there

II
I don't know what diseases
come down my line
when dentists and doctors ask
the old blood questions about family runnings
I tell them: I have no nose or eyes or mouth
to match, no spitting image or dead cert
my face watches itself in the glass

pull it out – the matter
matted as unoiled locks
my dread needs some grease to shine
these way past midnight hours
when the loneblood takes me in Brooklyn

I have my parents who are not of the same tree
and my brother that is not of my blood
though he is my bloodbrother and
you keep trying to make it matter
the blood, the tie, the passing down
generations

I am like my mother and father
I have seeped in Scotland's flavours
sizzling oatcakes on the griddle

I am like the mother and father
who brought me up and taught me
not how to be Black but
how not to be grateful
and for that I am glad

we all have our contradictions
the ones with the mother's nose and father's eyes have them
the blood does not bind confusion
yet some nights in Brooklyn
I confess to my contradiction
I want to know the blood from whence I sprang

III
I know my blood
it is dark ruby red and
comes regular and I use Lillets
I know my blood
when I cut my finger
I know what my blood looks like

it is the well the womb
the fucking seed
some nights in Brooklyn
I am far enough away to wonder
what were their faces like
who were their grandmothers
what were the days like
passed in Scotland
the land I come from
the soil in my blood

These next three poems come from my first play *Chiaroscuro*, presented by the Theatre of Black Women in 1986. The play was about the conflicts of four very different black women and their struggle to communicate with each other.

Aisha's Poem

it is just the wondering
the small frail maybe
the pushing away
before it can settle –
I am like they are
terrified of plunging
into that unknown country
the landscape with no familiar trees or flowers
the vastness of the moors
the never endingness of earth rolling
fear can stop a dream beginning
and wondering is wandering in the dark
stranger's voice echoing
yearning for that other woman
to hold me close –
could I sink in her depth?

it is the terror of beginnings
where the end cannot be envisaged
malicious words sitting on the edge
of my tongue where *I want* is smothered,
the terror of endings.

And the family, the family
what would they say?
Knowing anyway that I could say nothing
the emptiness of the unspoken years
how long could I live a lie
how long would the air stifle me in that closet?
yet the smell of an unwanted husband's breath
in the morning might make me
long   for those uncertain moors

And my landscape
is coloured in browns and reds;
she walks firm steps over it
I envy her
the way she's making history
whilst she walks; the implications of the foot
steps left behind
I follow them sink into shapes
a wood pigeon calls at dawn
light's uncertainty creates morning shadows.
I watch her go
the sturdy black woman walking
can just see her dark hair swing
I want to go with her
I want to go with her

But I've heard there are demons
that wait in morning shadows and
bloodhounds cry for   destruction

love might be just past
the weeping willow that's wept for years

so might death or shame
might hang from a Maple tree

whatever it is that's out there
it has no name or country

I am looking for a land
the belly and the brown

This morning I woke with the wood pigeon
I longed for the fresh air to
howl in my body, I wandered not
trusting how far I could go:
I saw her   before me
she must have felt me
she turned round; I stopped.

I wanted to go and meet her
I had so many questions I wanted to ask
but the terror that asking means wanting
and wanting can last forever
froze both of us
till we were stark silhouettes
captured by the twilight.

Yomi's Poem

I just pictured it blue
not the blue of the sea
but the blue of the blues
and bruises
how could anyone be happy
that way touching the very core
of anti-creation how could
someone love unnatural
like the last rays of sun
shine how could she feel hot
for she and want the heat on her back
like the pounding midday sun
opening the pores for the sweat to run
and I pictured it ugly
like the ugliness of something
you don't want to look at
imagining one might accost me
in the Ladies restroom
as soon as I heard Lesbian
I saw ugly and blue and lonely
and not being able to get
The Real Thing
and a tall angular looking woman
white with men's things on
too much hair around the mouth
and always on the prowl
she was so lonely
would die lonely
never knowing any kind of love
because lesbian and love
could not come together
like man and woman
I pictured ugly and lonely
(that was my only bit of sympathy)

and I couldn't see anyone
or smiles and softness and need
like Beth and Opal
looking good together
dark eyes lit by the fire in her
dark eyes sparkling at the woman in her
dark eyes dancing out the need of time
I looked at Beth and Opal
and I looked at my old pictures
I had to get out those albums
and go over the years.

Opal's Poem

If I could tear it up
the fear that wears no soft gloves
banish all the what ifs
and twenty years from now
where will I be
– how do dykes grow old?
I have this picture of Beth and I
loving all the finds
maturing like a good wine
love keeping us warm

whenever I see it —
love stretched over years
with plenty left to spread
I butcher the picture with my carving knife
and she is suddenly dead.
I am at her funeral
and no one there   knows what we meant to each other
and all her remaining relatives wonder
who is the sobbing woman in the dark coat
at the back with a pew to herself?

The picture makes me want to say now
and forever my name
tell them all where my loving lies
yet I stil turn my insides out
when I imagine what they would say
the old school friends, the old Home friends
the nurses the doctors and all the anonymous
who should mean Nothing
but might carry a knife
might follow me home
might write graffiti on my wall

I want to banish it all
the dread that keeps all hours
and let me live my life
and let me live my love
and let me love my life

MARILYN HACKER: My most recent book, *Love, Death, and the Changing of the Seasons* (Arbor House, 1986), is a narrative in sonnets chronicling the passionate, brief relationship of an older woman and a younger one. I am also the author of *Assumptions* (Knopf, 1985), *Taking Notice* (Knopf, 1980), *Separations* (Knopf, 1976), and *Presentation Piece* (Viking, 1974). I live in New York and Paris; my work has most recently appeared in Great Britain in *Ambit* and in the *London Magazine*. I am editor of the feminist literary magazine *13th Moon*.

Towards Autumn

Mid-September, and I miss my daughter.
I sit out on the terrace with my friend,
talking, with morning tea, coffee, and bread,
about another woman, and her mother,
who survived heroism; her lover
who will have to. I surprise myself

with language; lacking it, don't like myself
much. I owe a letter to my daughter.
Thinking of her's like thinking of a lover
I hope will someday grow to be a friend.
I missed the words to make friends with my mother.
I pull the long knife through the mound of bread,

spoon my slice with cherry preserves, the bread
chewy as meat beneath, remind myself
I've errands for our ancient patron, mother
of dramas, hard mother to a daughter
twenty years my senior, who is my friend,
who lives in exile with a woman lover

also my friend, three miles from here. A lover
of good bread, my (present) friend leaves this bread
and marmalades *biscottes*. To have a friend
a generation older than myself
is sometimes like a letter for my daughter
to read, when she can read: What your mother

left undone, women who are not your mother
may do. Women who are not your lover
love you. (That's to myself, and my daughter.)

We take coffee- and tea-pot, mugs, jam jars, bread
inside, wash up. I've work, hours by myself.
Beyond the kitchen, in her room, my friend

writes, overlooking the same hills. Befriend
yourself: I couldn't have known to tell my mother
that, unless I'd learned it for myself.
Until I do. Friendship is earned. A lover
leaps into faith. Earthbound women share bread;
make; do. Cherry compote would please my daughter.

My daughter was born hero to her mother;
found, like a lover, flawed; found, like a friend,
faithful as bread I'd learn to make myself.

Iva's Pantoum

We pace each other for a long time.
I packed my anger with the beef jerky.
You are the baby on the mountain. I am
in a cold stream where I led you.

I packed my anger with the beef jerky.
You are the woman sticking her tongue out
in a cold stream where I led you.
You are the woman with spring water palms.

You are the woman sticking her tongue out.
I am the woman who matches sounds.
You are the woman with spring water palms.
I am the woman who copies.

You are the woman who matches sounds.
You are the woman who makes up words.
You are the woman who copies
her cupped palm with her fist in clay.

I am the woman who makes up words.
You are the woman who shapes
a drinking bowl with her fist in clay.
I am the woman with rocks in her pockets.

I am the woman who shapes.
I was a baby who knew names.
You are the child with rocks in her pockets.
You are the girl in a plaid dress.

You are the woman who knows names.
You are the baby who could fly.
You are the girl in a plaid dress
upside-down on the monkey bars.

You are the baby who could fly
over the moon from a swinging perch
upside-down on the monkey bars.
You are the baby who eats meat.

Over the moon from a swinging perch
the feathery goblin calls her sister.
You are the baby who eats meat
the bitch wolf hunts and chews for you.

The feathery goblin calls her sister:
"You are braver than your mother.
The bitch wolf hunts and chews for you.
What are you whining about now?"

You are braver than your mother
and I am not a timid woman:
what are you whining about now?
My palms itch with slick anger,

and I'm not a timid woman.
You are the woman I can't mention;
my palms itch with slick anger.
You are the heiress of scraped knees.

You are the woman I can't mention
to a woman I want to love.
You are the heiress of scraped knees:
scrub them in mountain water.

To a woman, I want to love
women you could turn into,
scrub them in mountain water,
stroke their astonishing faces.

Women you could turn into
the scare mask of Bad Mother
stroke their astonishing faces
in the silver-scratched sink mirror.

The scare mask of Bad Mother
crumbles to chunked, pinched clay,
sinks in the silver-scratched mirror.
You are the Little Robber Girl, who

crumbles the clay chunks, pinches
her friend, gives her a sharp knife.
You are the Little Robber Girl, who
was any witch's youngest daughter.

Our friend gives you a sharp knife,
show how the useful blades open.
Was any witch's youngest daughter
golden and bold as you? You run and

show how the useful blades open.
You are the baby on the mountain. I am
golden and bold as you. You run and
we pace each other for a long time.

Corona
—for Kim Vaeth

You're flying back, weighted with half the books
that piled the work-table and the night-table.
They bulk your rucksack. You gum on a label,
consign it, while our eyes condense three weeks'
talk, silence, touch: relief, regret. It looks
like complicity. Friends, with a third friend,
I put my hand on your nape; you put your hand
in my back pocket. I kiss, first, both cheeks,
surprise you on your mouth. Your flight's called. I
watch you, helmed with departure, stubborn, brave
in cream shirt, lilac trousers, suede shoes, tie
the next tan, turn, glisten, go. Concave
space takes you, the cord's cut. We leave. I crave
uncomplicated quiet, and the sky.

Uncomplicated quiet, and the sky
a Marian mantle through the car window.
I think of all the things I'll never know.
"I wish I was older," the young girl said. "Why?"
"So I would know more." You and she and I
spanned twenty years among us. While you drove
serpent curves through vineyards and olive groves,
she read *The Bell Jar*, till we stopped to buy
Chianti at a *cave*, upturned the bell
concrete slab on pillars we saw boys make
lolloping dives from. You swim to it, break
thigh-high from the water, stretch to it, are
pendant by your wet arms, straining to pull
yourself up by them, drop, splash, leap again
determined from the water, less playful
now, challenged. You fall back. After ten
tries, you heave your leg over, stand, know I've
watched. I photograph your offhand dive.

Watched, I photograph your offhand dive.
How to depict attention that surveys
ground for reflexive confidence. Delays
are legion. When I navigate, you drive
home that indecision makes you arrive
exhausted anywhere. The hand belays
the rope to you's not mine. After a day's
mileage, Motown, nineteen-sixty-five;
we sing the car the last dark miles: "You can't
hurry love." We're almost what's almost home
to me. The constellated coast invokes
those road blues I'll sing myself, revenant
on airport buses when, again alone,
I'm flying back, weighted with half the books.
If I fail friendship, what felicity
left? Words crystallize despite our lives, select
emblems from hesitations and suspect
feelings. I coaxed your questioning, oblique,
till words undid what they had done. We speak
our pieces: peace. Plural, and amical,
we crossed the Arno, walked beyond the wall.

We cross the Arno, walk beyond the wall
up a steep wooded hill I climbed before
with another woman, hand in hand.
Now we hold hands, too, meaning something more
and less than "sex". At the ramparts, we stand
looking down sungilt waves of clay roof-tile
tender in late light slanted, now, toward Fall.
We separate ourselves from day-trip style
tourists, though we are tourists after all.
We need a breather from the personal.
Facts permit us touch. You rest your head on
my lap while I praise Suzanne Valadon.
Fatigue relaxes to repose in your
tanned shoulders, opulent and muscular.

Tanned shoulders, opulent and muscular,
power exuberant strokes. The choppy lake
frames, then conceals, your dolphin play. You take
a deep breath and submerge, then surface, far
away, all shining. There's a rectangular
to shining tulips where the garnet wine
perfumed our morning. Weight in the palm, see, smell,
taste: our three mouths contemplated fine
meditations of ancient earth, as well
considered as just measures for a line.

Considered as just measures for a line,
sound more than sense determines words I choose;
invention mutes intention. If the shoes
you bought were grey suede clogs, size thirty-nine,
if we sang passion's matins and compline,
I'm story-telling. Reading poetry
we expect truth, you said, and I agree.
Truth, in particulars, I can define.
They're brown, your oxfords, and size forty-one;
two nuns, watching over another nun
through a night of fever, could not have kept
their limbs more ordered than we did; we slept
apart, together: facile franchise, whose
unsubtle truth can blanket subtlety.

Unsubtle truth can blanket subtlety.
In the next room, you slept in our guest-friend bed.
Where I wrote, your pad sat, pen-marked. I read
that morning, what, that night, you'd thought of me.
I wished I could evaporate, could be
anywhere else. I thought "Ingratitude,"
and flinched, while Tuscan light ignored my mood.

Grief, and I want to take it up in you;
joy, and I want to spend it all inside
you; fear, and you are the place I can hide.
Courage is what leaves me brave enough to
turn you around and tell you what to do
to me, after. Rivers, and downstream glide
I; we breathe together. You look, or I'd
get scared, but you're watching while you take me through
the deep part, where I find you, where you need
to know I do know where, know how to drive
the point home. Wit: you get the point and flat
statement of a gift of tongues. I get
up, and you get me down, get lost, you lead
me home, or I take you, and we both arrive.

First, I want to make you come in my hand
while I watch you & kiss you, and if you cry,
I'll drink your tears, while with my whole hand, I
hold your drenched loveliness contracting. And
after a breath, I want to make you full
again, & wet. I want to make you come
in my mouth like a storm. No tears now. The sum
of your parts is my whole beautiful
chart of the constellations — your left breast
in my mouth again. You know you'll have to be
your age. As I lie beside you, cover me
like a gold cloud, hands everywhere, at last
inside me where I trust you, then your tongue
where I need you. I want you to make me come.

Canzone

Consider the three functions of the tongue:
taste, speech, the telegraphy of pleasure,
are not confused in any human tongue;
yet, sinewy and singular, the tongue
accomplishes what, perhaps, no other organ
can. Were I to speak of giving tongue,
you'd think two things at least; and a cooked tongue,
sliced, on a plate, with caper sauce, which I give
my guest for lunch, is one more, to which she'd give
the careful concentration of her tongue
twice over, to appreciate the taste
and to express—it would be in good taste—

a gastronomic memory the taste
called to mind, and mind brought back to tongue.
There is a paucity of words for taste:
sweet, sour, bitter, salty. Any taste,
however multiplicitous its pleasure,
complex its execution (I might taste
that sauce ten times in cooking, change its taste
with herbal subtleties, chromatic organ
tones of clove and basil, good with organ
meats) must be described with those few taste-
words, or with metaphors, to give
my version of sensations it would give

a neophyte, deciding whether to give
it a try. She might develop a taste.
(You try things once; I think you have to give
two chances, though, to know your mind, or give
up on novelties.) Your mother tongue
nurtures, has the subtleties which give

flavor to words, and words to flavor, give
the by no means subsidiary pleasure
of being able to describe a pleasure
and recreate it. Making words, we give
the private contemplations of each organ
to the others, and to others, organ-

ize sensations into thoughts. Sentient organ-
isms, we symbolize feeling, give
the spectrum (that's a symbol) each sense organ
perceives, by analogy, to others. Disorgan-
ization of the senses is an acquired taste
we all acquire; as speaking beasts, its organ-
ic to our discourse. The first organ
of acknowledged communion is the tongue
(tripartite diplomat, which after tonguing a less voluble expressive organ
to wordless efflorescences of pleasure
offers up words to reaffirm the pleasure).

That's a pirmary difficulty: pleasure
means something, and something different, for each organ;
each person, too. I may take exquisite pleasure
in boiled eel, or blancmange—or not. One pleasure
of language is making known what not to give.
And think of a bar of lavender soap, a pleasure
to see and, moistened, rub on your skin, a pleasure
especially to smell, but if you taste
it (though smell is most akin to taste)
what you experience will not be pleasure;
you almost retch, grimace, stick out your tongue,
slosh rinses of ice water over your tongue.

But I would rather think about your tongue
experiencing and transmitting pleasure
to one or another multi-sensual organ
—like memory. Whoever wants to give
only one meaning to that, has untutored taste.

JOY HOWARD would really prefer to remain anonymous, but can't square that with wanting to have her poems published. Having opened the closet door thus far, she will admit to being in her mid-forties, living and working in London, having a white middle-class English Catholic background and education, three sons, three sisters, some wonderful friends, strong views on 'the problem of men', and a deep committment to getting on with life against all the odds, which don't seem to shorten as time goes on. She has been engaged in political struggle in and around the Women's Movement since 1978, and has been a lesbian since 1980, and often wonders why it took her so long. She has been writing poetry also since 1980, and doesn't believe in coincidences.

Prufrock Revisited

Oh yes I once went in for
measuring my life with coffee spoons
and toast and tea
I did not dare presume nor want
to play Prince Hamlet
walked on beaches never reaching for
the red-brown sea.

(supposing she should say no that is
not what I meant
not it at all)

but there was time indeed
grown older now I wear
the bottoms of my trousers rolled like
any other dyke and eat
my daily peach
you see I hear
the mermaids singing each to each
and know
they sing for me.

'What, a Play Toward!'

Funny wasn't it   how you
and I   like actors
teased and joked away our time
going for laughs
with now and then a little edge
to it – of competition?
rivalry?   or was it some
sharper arrow
deflecting from our fathers'
chambered wall?

A good script though   well learned
(with just an occasional prompt)
reliable   could have
a long run
always all right
on the night

What puckish demon
was it then that made me
call you 'darling'
(did you hear it?)
bound to blunt you   a stone
falling by accident
dangerous   a gap
that had to be closed

Oh yes   stone walls
still need repairing
in this country   built
with chinks just wide enough
for moonshine
not the hoarse-whispered blurtings
of a blundering Thisbe
with a fear
of forgetting her lines
and half an eye
for Hippolyta

Always in trouble with my timing
lion stage-fright snarling
in the wings
forgive me then if I
(in rustic confusion)
sometimes wished
to toss the script and leap the wall
and exit moonshine
with a kiss?

p.m.

Sunday and the Underground
is suddenly filled
with children
sleepy mostly in
the hot and stuffy air
young mothers gazing
into space   their arms
in automatic careless
careful circles
around the placid bodies
idly twisting
childish locks of hair
and thinking
of the blessed peace
at least another
six stops
before it all starts up
again

Let me O let me live
by you a little longer
not disperse
my spirit   nurse
me   lead me kindly on
till I am somewhat stronger
nothing worse:
the Universe
is full of stars that change
their courses   though in danger
do not curse
the all perverse
nature of Fate that keeps
them permanently stranger
for they know
that each must go
from near kind light of friends
that each must be the changer

So I will leave you   yet
keep this one small spark alight:
that your star
however far
the journey   or how faint
remain constant in my sight

The Pearl Hunter

I'm diving deeper
soon
there'll be no heading
back for the surface
and I
merwoman
weaving among the weeds
haunting the coral caves
with my soundless cry
and sightless tears
will mourn
for the sport of the shallows

Gertrude Stein

Her quality
is never strained
it falls
as crystal hail
on shuttered windows
waking us sharply from our comfortable
winter's sleep
flies
like fiery sparks shot
from a burning branch
dissolving where they land our covering
of shape-concealing snow
revealing at each small melting point
the form beneath
feels
like a shower of iron filings
each tiny missile strong and hard
pricking with its insistent rain
complacency making us
a magnet for her words
rises
like bubbles in a glass
of sparkling burgundy
tickling our senses till we must
give ourselves over to inebriate laughter
as we drink our fortune
in the future
she so richly left us

CAROLINE GRIFFIN: I was born in the Midlands in 1950 and have three sisters. I have lived in a women's house for the past 13 years while working as an English teacher committed to anti-sexist education in a boys' comprehensive school. My daughter (I am a non-biological mother) who is nearly seven has one hand and a short arm, lots of ideas and a good sense of humour. Two years ago I began co-writing plays with Maro Green. *More* (to be published by Methuen 1987) toured London successfully in 1986 – *The Memorial Gardens* (produced by Gay Sweatshop) opens in 1987. *More* explored hidden disability as an intelligent strategy for survival, not just a problem – my life, since I have been afraid to be alone ('agoraphobic') for several years. My daughter, my friends and my lover continue to support and inspire me. My mother, Sylvia, died recently. She first taught me to care for books and was a writer, too – thank you.

I
We are pressed so close
my head is earth   our lips are earth
Oh speak to me only with your breasts
and feel the intimate mud and rubble
of our bodies turning in the stuck boundaries
of this bed   we have talked too much
and now must hunt through eye-sockets –
contact through bone –
whether the light is there.

'There has to be something' –
I clutch at you   there has to be something
which outlasts some rub of the everyday.
And then I push away your hand
make you a woman of straw because
I have more things to say. Oh please
alter my argument.

II
Pale light behind the linen blinds
I clamber from my dreams
your chair   your desk
cradle your warm and tender body –
early morning touches.

At last the fire is held –
the coals breathe pale wood flickers.
Each flame needs feeding I think
building intricacies of sticks
cut small enough for this place.
And there have been decisions
where to put our clothes our books,
making this a home.

Or together on a coach
your head in my lap
on the naughty kids' back seat –
against the engine's hum the bucking wheels
I sing lullabies and stroke your hair
through country we don't notice.
This is our home together.

III
Do not adjust the shape of the fire too much.
Yet I presume to know where the logs fit
where the flames lick.
When the fire falls watch out
hot coals and scorched wood
tumble from the grate –
and both of us have said out dreams before
with all the naked hope of now
and some regret is part of what we bring
some part of why I forget to love.

IV
Pale light into my dreams.
Your warm and loving body
senses mine   sees my thoughts –
it seems trust is your interest
to go on putting your hand next to mine
to hold the same thread
in the labyrinthine home we move through.

'If our lives are not like our dreams
then what's the point of living?'

She suspects the day of greyness
this is not commonplace but
frequent   gets up
holds the ordinary day in her heart
for a moment – it leaps and kicks
this is familiar not ordinary
she puts the day down
picks herself up
tries to breathe
this is habitual but hard
breathes out   suspects the day
of holding up her life
longs to be held
holds tight to her books and her letters
repeats her name
suspects her bag of weighing more than she does
relies on it
her ordinary life
hopes her heart will go on beating
hopes her life will not mind her questions.

'No exorciser harm thee!
  Nor no witchcraft charm thee!
Ghosts unlaid forbear thee!
  Nothing ill come near thee!'
                    Shakespeare

It is time for our shouts now   to grasp
with the anger of feet striking the pavement
to kiss   with the blunt courage of faces
dividing the wind. This time my body
presses down to prove our goodness   turns
to shake them off – faster – with you here
I touch the pain of places pushed away
hold your thighs   in the twist of reaching to
where we want.

Our shouts now – hearing the clash of metal
recognising armour. So we fight out our love
holding tight   knowing our hands are threatened.
No soft breaking open this   the rapt body listens
reached as far as my defences.

Here am I   a blunt stone in a stream.
Lie on top of me. I divert them
they divide and run. Now this grip
hardens to hold you while we fly
fast in the teeth of
all which makes our women's hands taut
showing the line of muscles drawn to an edge.

I do not lack the idea of loving,
that person I want to be, given some air.
I have walked under the stars with you
and felt like flying   but

here is an old feeling –
getting close to someone
is a possible risk of my safety.
I can't fly. I can scarcely own taking more time
            to feel your arms around me longer.

If I could start again, now
asserting my right to be loved
a child in this body rightfully here –

I would not thank you for holding me
I would give up   thanks
such gratitude burns   what have I done
to feel grateful for touching
I would give up   absolution.

my anger will burn it away.

Without this to start from
the child   the green space
the rest is nothing just
a struggle to be in your imagination
somewhere else in mine.

I feel so heavy,
and speak of these things
as though someone would disagree.

I need to lie   let the quiet build up
my hands open to space
my body flat   be with me
the quiet builds up   I can breathe deeply
feel a stream inside me trickling
I am   and sometimes you are there too.

The woman as a phoenix . . .

Well her ribs are sometimes taut
like a bird's   when there is pain
womens hands search beneath her shoulder blades
there may be wings   she is ready for flight often but
her medium is earth not air
she may lie on it
with the pain of all she has not said
beating in her ribs

there is fierce heat   she walks
to find water   her feet on cold stone
and shaking she tries to let the heat
pass through to earth   regret
the self alone in such a situation.

there is fierce holding
to the place the body the night
she has smoothed her body from crown to toe
her pubic hair warm – a lying damp
between bone hips the brown line from
navel to hair   this body that she will die with

there is no holy fire to make her anew
'again and again' is a heavy weight and she
sometimes forgets there is not one of her
her spiritual crises are often in the night
beside the washbasin   give her respect
it makes a fragile bridge between the night
and day   she will grip tightly just as
long as it takes.

JUDITH BARRINGTON: I am forty-two years old and have been active in feminist and lesbian communities since 1972. Before that I was a lesbian looking for a context.

Since moving to the U.S. in 1976, I have made a living for myself as a freelance writer, been part of creating an annual writing workshop for women in the Oregon mountains, and published a book of poetry.

Although feminism has given me a context and a voice, it has not provided me with the craft worthy of my material. As a frequent reviewer, I see my dilemma reflected in the work of many feminist writers, who are understandably suspicious of traditional literary standards, yet seek the power that greater technical skills would bring to our writing. In actively pursuing these skills I feel I have finally found my work.

Four Days in Spain

In December 1963, the cruise-ship Lakonia caught fire
near the Canary Isles. Close to a hundred people died,
some during the initial panic, as crew and passengers
tried to escape in lifeboats, and others, like my mother
and father, several days later when the fire forced those
who were left without lifeboats to abandon the ship.

These are memories of a journey my sister and I
made to Gibraltar, where our parents' bodies had been
taken for burial. We planned to visit the graves and
arrange for a permanent marker in the cemetery.

My sister flew to meet me in Barcelona, where I had
been working for the summer. I was 20; she was 31.

1
Plaza Catalũna, Barcelona

We sit at a plastic table close to the kerb,
fending off lorries and madcap Seats,
southern relatives of the Fiat. It's hard to talk.
Mopeds whirr past like slender sewing machines—
the girls still ride behind, sidesaddle.
This is late summer, 1964.

My sister fresh from the airport is crumpled
in the respectable navy blue of sudden transitions
while I lounge cool in my tan and sea tones
ordering drinks and telling her how we locals
despise the tourists. If she wonders
how I have become this in three months

she says nothing. We sip sweet martini
poured from miniature bottles
over one small ice cube with a splash of soda.
The road map hangs over the round table
as we trace with our fingers
the coast road south, adding up the miles

between little hatpin symbols
stuck into the towns—round red blobs
hiding moorish and modern, mosaic and concrete
where donkeys in straw hats will be standing,
I know, under lofty palms, ears protruding
to the hum of flies and the languid sea.

"My god" says my sister "I'm only halfway there"
as she looks at the red line we will drive together
and I gaze out past the glassy bank towers
at the Plaza' fountains, deprived of splashing
by the harsh traffic, their tulip shapes carved
in the perfect symmetry of a suburban hedge sculpture.

"I hope the boys will be all right" she frets,
home ties still more real than the journey ahead.
Over in the square the Spanish grass is unwalkable
its blades broad and sharp like razors.
My drink as usual tastes like cough mixture.
We never mention the purpose of the trip.

2
Snapshot at Cullera

Café con leche for breakfast
with frothy milk
in huge thick cups
and Spanish croissants—
more solid less flaky
than the French ones.
The new hotel balcony
aspires to elegance,
though the long, boring beach
with its oil-slick-grey ocean
hardly helps
on this tired morning.
Pale sunshine
cool in the photograph
gives no hint
of the fierce blaze
that soon will throw aside
the morning fog,
insinuate its stifling breath
into cringing corners,
grope behind barrels of lentils
in dark epicerías,
and probe each private fold
of a million prickly pears.

In the snapshot
my sister looks more at home now
with her faded red shirt
and slacks
trying to remember
the few Spanish words
she learned as a child.

Her prescription sunglasses
come to diabolical points—
already old-fashioned
in 1964.

At the end of the beach
on a low headland
squats "Papaluna"—
grey lighthouse
inexplicably named
"Father moon"
She thinks the name
endearing.
I don't tell her
what I think.

3
On the Road

The sandscape unfolds on the windows of the car
like back projection in the studio, images
racing past the shell of a vehicle
hung with microphones, blown full
of artificial life by the wind machine—
backdrop for sporadic conversation.

My sister talks of her garden, fruit trees
and endless runner beans as we bump
over cobbles through some ragged pueblo.
She will always have a tiled lobby or sunroom
full of wellingtons and raincoats
for her walks through dripping woods.

Cabo de la Nao pokes its nose out
towards Mallorca, Ibiza, and Menorca
islands among the sunspots hovering
like white-hot snowflakes that burn our eyes . . .
and I see her pottering like our mother
tall and stooped, picking peas, trug in hand.

We speak of her world: Scarlatti, Bach,
the new Dolmetsch harpsichord, the rabbits
and the dogs. A woman in a house of men now
she sprang, like Athena, from our father's head,
understood the workings of his mind
as I never could—never cared to.

Long ago, the house was quiet when she left—
not that we'd really talked, though I'd wished we could;
her new grand piano had murmured in my ear
intimate sister secrets never said . . .
alone in the quiet house with just a dream horse
and parents who were tired of the young.

On the road south, the beaches fill with tourists—
a rash of blushing bodies, and speedboats slice
the perfect green water as sweat pours
down our necks and we munch on fat black grapes
spitting careless seeds into the backdrop.
We both know it is safer to talk of her world.

4
What is Not Said

We are travelling southwest.
My sister won't drive
since here the traffic
moves on the right.
Even on the left she's slow—
just like our mother,
though of course I don't say so
now that she's dead.

My sister does not ask how I spent the summer
or where I got the silver link bracelet
or how it feels to live in Spain alone.

We are travelling southwest
The sun on her side
burns her cheek and neck
to an angry flush
despite the silk scarf
wedged in the window
filtering the fierce rays
through its turquoise sheen.

I do not tell my sister the summer was wine and sex,
the bracelet a gift from an old man, and being lonely here
is better than there because strangers are more comfort.

We are travelling southwest.
as the road climbs away from the sea
among gnarled and faded olive trees.
Cicadas cry so loud
we hear them above
the car's whining effort
and the lust of dusty men
hissing: "Oíga! Guapa—Guapa!"

We do not ask each other "how have you been—
all these months with no parents?" or "do you remember?"
Five hundred miles to the grave but we do not say so.

We are merely travelling southwest.

5
Lorca

At Alicante our road leaves the coast,
drops its facade of wealth and climbs
through dust and boulders like a moonscape.
Careful people look over their shoulders
when they speak of the war
and Franco's rule is not softened
by those beachfront tourist dollars.
Women in black keep their heads down—
circle the rambla under the arched colonnade
always in the shadows. Our hotel
has dusty sofas on each landing
where maids sit darning blankets with
neat even stitches and brilliant blue
ceramic tiles peer through
the abundant foliage of sombre aspidistras
gloomy as trees. Heavy shutters
deny the morning sun.

I wake late in my feather bed
with sheets starched like a nurse.
My sister opens one shutter, pales
as the sun strikes the scarlet stain
on the pillow. My treacherous nose—
a pool of dried blood—
too eloquent—dangerous.

6
The End of the Road

Turning west at Almería the road meets the beach
and we stop over and over to run and dive
breaking silence with squeals as we smack the sea
still in our clothes, then stagger back to the car,
cool till the hot wind dries us out again.
Sometimes we sit on the beach, eating melon

till it runs down our chins and our clothes
and skins are sticky with juice, gritty with sand.
We refill the wine bottle daily for five pesetas
at dark stores hung with chorizo and everywhere
children hold out their hopeful palms
and bold graffiti sing praise to the anarchists.

Tomorrow we'll reach Gibraltar with massive ships,
black marketeers, flea-bitten apes on The Rock.
Tomorrow we'll scan the lines of black wooden crosses—
fading, powdered with dust, weeds at their feet.
We'll soberly search for our two, the ground will be hot,
and in ranks of identical markers, two will be ours.

But today we start on songs from our serial childhoods
and harmonize on *The Lass of Richmond Hill*;
rolling our eyes to the doleful *Who is Sylvia?*
we giggle and groan as we travel, always southwest.
Today we are sisters, lost in a rare common world,
but we never mention the purpose of the trip.

ANDREA FREUD LOEWENSTEIN: I am a writer and teacher, now back in the USA (after two years of living in London). In my teaching, I try to help women who have been denied their voice to get it back. In my writing, I concentrate most on fiction: I am the author of *This Place*, set in a women's prison, and am hoping soon to finish a new book about an american lesbian mother and her daughter, set in London. I have also been writing poetry ever since I could write. I think of my poems as a kind of music which need to be heard to be enjoyed best, so I hope some of you will read them aloud.

Two Women

(1)
In childhood
a year or two
makes so much difference.
A friend, only two years older
seems grownup.
A mother dresses and moves her child
through its early life
like a little doll
making the legs walk.
Years later, especially in the case of an unmarried
    daughter
mother and child often seem to be
the same age.
An old woman sits
with an older woman.
They could be sisters.

(2)
My mother had to leave her country early
traveling on a bicycle
behind her mother
"The Nazis were shooting at us"
she told me.
"I was always with her, always.
I could never get away.
Once in america I left her
as soon as I could."
This story is only a few bare
pictures.
I never found out the right dates, the correct places of
embarkment
or destination.

(3)
In an early photo, saved somehow,
my mother is dressed in embroidered silk Chinese
    pajamas.
They are on the beach, at Grado.
She has dark straight hair, bangs, slanted eyes and
looks more like a little Chinese girl than what she is –
a Jew.
"She used to show me off to her friends," my mother said.
"I hated those pajamas."
She has protruding teeth in this photo, braces in the
    later ones.
Her mother had to cut them off in the flight
when there were no more orthodontists.

(4)
This story too, is indistinct.
Did she really love or hate those pajamas?
Was it her mother who cut the braces off?
Whichever way I tell it, it will be wrong.
"I never told you that. No no
You must have made it up."
And its true that the scissors I see Oma use
to cut my mother's braces off
are the blunt-edged scissors we got in school.
They smell of paste
as they approach my mouth.
Maybe I did make it up
after all.

(5)
In early photos I have straight brown hair in bangs.
I wear sturdy corduroy pants, not for
show.
I stare solemnly into the camera.
My expression is suspicious for such a small child
as if I am watching carefully
to see what she will do next.
In a later photo I am wearing
a grey silk dress, bought over her protests
for dancing school.
The crowning glory is an artificial rose.
My expression is one of subdued triumph.
I wear braces.
No one is chasing me.
I know this memory
is true.

(6)
My mother and I sit in her house
two not-young women with protruding teeth,
lined faces, curly hair.
There are no children here, hers are grown
and I am getting past the age.
Cozy as two sisters
we drink tea,
read our books,
exchange stories,
dreams.

(7)
In my mother's dream
she walks through a great hotel
looking, looking
for the right room.
Her friends cannot help her.
Her husband moves off
without listening or looking back
and rides the elevator *up*
to an unknown destination.
All night she looks and looks
for the right room,
for *her* room.
She doesn't give up.
In the morning she is sitting on a bench
when her mother comes by.
"What is this I hear?" she asks angrily.
"They say you are wanted by the police."

(8)
In my dream I walk down a long dusty road
somewhere in the South.
I am a bad girl, I want only to escape
but there are no bearable choices,
only the camp behind with its unspeakable tortures
and my mother's house ahead
where she sits sewing white dresses for a multitude of
    baby dolls
Even in my dream I know my mother has important
    work to do.
I wonder why she sits and sews for these frozen-limbed
    dolls
in this house that is not my home
but is the only place
I recognize.

(9)
In childhood
a year or two
makes so much difference.
A friend, only two years older
seems grownup.
Years later, especially in the case of an unmarried
    daughter
mother and child often seem to be
the same age.
A woman sits
with an older woman.
They could be sisters.

In Answer to your question, What do I want?

Like that time I told you about —
walking back from the library
by the frozen lake
in the midwestern cold at 2AM
feeling every step
every
step.
Yes, I was in love then, No I don't remember
don't you see it doesn't matter
with whom?
Or like when I used to stay up all night and drive home
as the morning turned white.
It was summertime, I had a convertible then,
the top would be down.
On the home stretch
I'd be the only one on the road
and all the way down Main Street
as far as I could see
nothing, nothing,
but green lights.

Replay

Take back one giant step, don't cheat.
Replay another way.
Truth, dare, promise to repeat
after me, now say:
Never like two cats have we
licked each other with rough tongues,
nor moved through that amazing sea.
You have not called, I have not clung.
Replay it clothed, un-learn, un-know.
I'll dress you from the outside in.
A vest on top, a shirt below.
Now say: I never knew your skin.
Two spins, face front, replay,
but this time stress
that when you, trembling, turned to me
I turned away
and never answered yes.

Living In The War Zone
(Cambridge, Massachusetts, USA, 1980)

the world is getting too
Dangerous. Outside
boy children ride screaming
bike wheels rearing over
broken bottle-glass crashing to
break.
DYKE, DYKE they yell
every time
I come out
till I want to twist their necks like chickens
off.
Your anger begins to haunt me.
I see it everywhere,
accusing.
Firecrackers or guns
explode all day outside.
"Why are you *doing* this to me,"
you scream,
"WHY?"
At school
the bad little girls tell me
bout the party
where three or four fucked one
in the bathroom.
"She too high to know
who-all been in her pussy.
The room stink, after.
When the mens bring in their guns is time to leave."

I am afraid of what you say to me
when your voice grows hard
and your face turns into someone else's —
someone I don't know.
All the bad little girls get pregnant and have other
little girls whom they leave alone till they scream
so loud the Welfare come and they get
took away.
In the gay bar someone is banging her lover's head on
     the floor.
"That's for what you did to me last night!"
I read they found some woman's parts in a black plastic
garbage bag it's Friday
time to take out the trash.
"DYKE" "DYKE."
Every man in the street with his hand in his pocket
is pulling out a gun and
I cannot even be gentle with you
whom I love more than anyone
in the world.

Fireboat

for Amy Hoffman, Cliff Island, Maine.

(On this small island when someone falls ill or is hurt,
the fireboat must come to transport them to the
hospital on the mainland.)

The fireboat rises huge
against the dark water
blinking its red and green lights,
nudging the dock
as in a dream where
what must be gone through, is.
We stand with the island watchers
as slowly, slowly – they send for the old man.
He arrives lying down
white and silent, hands folded neatly
on the stretcher's red blanket
and is lowered into the fire boat.
What's the matter, we ask,
and the watchers answer us, murmuring
Heart attack.
Heart. Attack.
Then they bring the old woman.
She arrives standing, smiling at us all.
Is it his wife, we ask
and the answer comes. No,
only a distant relative.
We wait for them to help her into the boat
but they point to the stretcher instead
and she lies down neatly, folding her hands
on the red blanket, and is lowered down.

The fireboat noses off
into the dark water,
the watchers disappear,
and you and I are left to walk back
to our house on this night island
at summer's end,
feeling for our footing on the dark path,
avoiding steadying touch.
It happened like a dream, I say
telling you the story of the evening
so that you will know, afterwards,
that you didn't make it up,
laying words as neat and purposeful as bricks
which vanish into the night
and do nothing to stop
our collision, which when it happens will be
as wordless as the fireboat,
nudging its way out and back,
disregarding our anxious questions,
Our plans.

These are two poems I found when teaching English as a Second Language.

Survival English

I am looking for a job.
Where is the bus stop?
My address is 362 Rindge Towers.
I have got no phone.
My name is Marie Joseph.
I am lost.
Can you show me where?

English Lesson

The verb to miss (in French, manquer)
I miss you now.
Yesterday I missed you.
It seems I have missed you for a long time.
When you were making love to her, I was missing you.
I would miss you even if I never saw you again.
I know I will miss you always.
Another use of the verb to miss (in French, rater)
I missed the bus.
You missed your chance.
We missed.

BERNARDINE EVARISTO: Born in London in 1959 to Nigerian and English parents. Working in theatre as a performer, playwright and drama tutor. I have been writing for several years a process of struggle and enlightenment as I reach out and within to find the root; the direct line to my ancestors. Plays written for and toured by Theatre of Black Women include *Tiger Teeth Clenched Not To Bite* ('83), *Silhouette* ('84) and *Pyeyucca* ('85), the latter two were co-written with Patricia Hilaire. More of my poems will shortly be published in *Charting the Journey* Sheba Feminist Publishers and the Black Woman Talk poetry anthology.

The Blonde in Buki

It was Christmas 1965 and the little girl Buki
was given a blonde dolly by her mother,
Belinda, is what she called her
with hair the colour of corn,
eyes that shone green,
wearing a pink frilly frock
with white slippers to match
Belinda became the Blonde in Buki.
The dolly was her fantasy and through her
she lived a life far removed from her own;

> Mirror, Mirror on the wall
> who is the fairest of them all?
> "Not you, little one, not you.
> Your skin too dark like the blackest night.
> Your hair too wild like the jungles of Africa.
> Your nose too flat like the plains of America.
> Your lips too big like the Amazon waters.
> Not you, little one, not you"

As time went by Buki grew up and away from dolls
so Belinda met her death one windy afternoon
and there on top of a bonfire, in all her glory,
she melted away, as the snow does for the sun,
but the dream lived on;

> Mirror, Mirror on the wall
> who is the fairest of them all?
> "Not you, little one, not you.
> Her skin as white as snowflakes in winter.
> Her hair as silky as the wings of a butterfly.
> Her lips as red as white rosebuds in June.
> Her nose as slender as the ski slopes of Italy.
> Not you, little one, not you."

Aged eleven and at her new school
Buki found Belinda reincarnate: Julie!
with long blonde hair, eyes of green
and a smile that melted a thousand hearts.
She could have walked straight off the
pages of Jackie magazine and was loved by all,

not that Buki hated her own looks, you understand
for when she looked into the mirror,
the image reflected the dream
and her own kinky hair was transformed
into fields of corn, her eyes shone green
and her smile melted a thousand hearts.

Olu-A-Day

Coal black marbles that tell a story
from the silver grey of night
to the bright dawning of morning
as this humming bird/Olu? shall we call
we call her, rolls over to rise
feeling the pain in her back
asking for help.

She glances into the mirror
registers the vivid lines
that begin to distinguish themselves
beneath the marbles.
Notice the unfocussed glaze
hiding, always hiding
hide the spirit
Ipita! Ipita!

Olu rises with slow languorous movements
feeling the nightmares of sleep
in the blades of her shoulders,
reaches for a cigarette
to bring in the day
that holds the woman who entered
and will not leave
nestling in her stomach
with luminous eyes that penetrate
and hide all the same,

and so with gentle soft stirrings
Olu washes and mundanes herself
around the house,
forget about breakfast,no inspiration
only the woman who refuses to leave
who plunders her silver quick brain
keeping her busy as she
rides the grey tarmac to work.

Near enough to be seen
but not to be touched
beckoning withdrawal and mistrust
holding fascination for Olu
whose coal black marbles now
know the reddening colour that
shades both their lives,

the woman whose eyes have not yet
been truly sought by Olu
who slips and slides
to avoid any everlasting gaze
whilst trying to cover up
the real feel of her red.

Tiger Teeth Clenched Not To Bite

Rock mounting rock
till head erect
sealed in by the skin of a rhino,

thoughts only of those handed down
tiger teeth clenched not to bite,

speak only when spoken to
though nobody said so
no volcanic eruptions tonight!

body lies languid
not on beach sun and sea
but absorbing its comforting enemy
that keeps lion at bay
not quite cat by the fireside
but one always returning
to the seat of luke warm heat,

the price you see is high
oh dear, oh my dear
no god to yield to
our souls our bodies
only ourselves
which is a lot to take on.

Sun Clouds Dry

Sun clouds dry
deep red orange red murram soil
compact rumbling with green grass
yellowed by sun god
tree's large swaying in no wind
country land for miles
mats interwoven many colours

bus packed full with bodies sweat
bus small mural inside
music throb american funk
old woman plays old instrument

African heritage shop
walking Masai man in old clothes
walking Masai monument
to culture dying
absorbed by movement of the west

dancers imported from bush
to make tourist money
make shillings to live
take it

pink Flamingos embroider Lake Nakuru
millions in natural habitat

no haven no cane rowed orange groved
pineappled farms glisten in sunlight
dream without rememberance
no human fantasy for our country
just a love for the land

sun sets behind wild ocean
coconut palms rampage in breeze
crickets begin night chorus
crickets a chorus
lizards a scamper
buzz a mosquito

sea laps to shore
as students massacred by military
ending peaceful sit-in protest
against political prisoners
become prisoners
some unliving
no idyll no haven

paradise lost in the Mathares valley
blood lost by challengers
blood lost by virgin girl children
as thorn trees stud the horizon
as train rolls into night
immovable and strange
as daughters sold to germans
in coastal town
women of Malindi
pay well for survival

one poem of Africa in me
one poem of Kenya in me
weighting my mind
like the swamps of the Sudd.

Flame Dance

As the flames danced in the reflection
of the brown mirrors
that let my world out,
and the day drawing to a close
unseen behind the living room curtains
that close the world out,

as the fire that smoulders unseen
by the tourist gazing blindly at the mirrors
that stoney stare emptiness,

and the child who cannot tell
but will laugh all the same
when my eye winks to create fun,
and the plants that know I mean well
though winter is winter,

as the woman who sits opposite
whose wild seas of eyes
penetrate and wash through the wood
that now cracks
to allow the waters in,
as you and I will find the strand
now missing, waiting to be caught.

You see as I watched the flames
dance before you, lady,
and the light in my eyes
tried to stifle the fire within
I knew that you knew,
though the telling would make no difference.

MARY DORCEY: was born in Dublin, Ireland. Active in the women's movement since 1972, she was a founder member of Irishwomen United, and the first Dublin lesbian group. She has lived and worked in France the U.S.A., England and Japan. She has been writing on and off since 1980, supporting herself by social welfare and part time work. Her first book of poetry *Kindling* was published by Onlywomen Press in 1982, since then her work has been anthologised in *The Virago Book of Women's Poetry*, *In the Pink* (The Women's Press) *Contemporary Poetry* (Oxford University Press), and a short story was published in *Girls Next Door* (The Women's Press).

She is currently living in the west of Ireland, completing a collection of short stories and working on a novel.

The Ordinary Woman

And again you ask me why –
Why don't I write a poem about
The ordinary woman?
Not the extreme, individual case,
But the normal woman, the average woman
The everyday woman.

The woman in the street
The woman in the field
The woman who works in a factory
The woman who works on a farm
The woman who has never heard of a factory
The woman who has never seen a field.

The woman who stays at home
The woman who has no home
The woman who raises children
The woman who can have no children
The woman who has too many children
The woman who wants no children.

The healthy woman the sick woman
The growing woman the dying woman
The menstruating woman the menopausal woman
The married woman the spinster woman
The woman on the make
The woman on the shelf.

The woman who works in a school
The woman who dropped out of school
The woman who never got into school.

The woman who works as a nurse
The woman who cooks for the nurse
The woman who cleans the kitchen

Where they cook for the nurse.
The woman who works in a shop everyday
The woman who shops every day
The woman who shops for food
The woman who shops for clothes, for perfume
The woman who shoplifts

For clothes, for perfume.
The woman who is paid to catch
The woman who does not pay
For clothes for food.
The career woman the poetess woman
The mother earth woman the charwoman

The amazon woman the society woman
The sportswoman the little woman
The woman who runs the woman who walks
The woman who is on the run
The woman who has never walked.
The woman who drives a car

The woman who drives her husbands car.
The pampered woman the kept woman
The sheltered woman the battered woman
The victimised woman the violent woman
The woman nobody wants
The woman who had it coming.

The woman who went sane
The woman who stayed mad
The woman who carries a gun
The woman who is shot by a gun
The woman with too much past
The woman with too little future.

The woman ahead of her times
The woman behind the times
The woman with no time.
The outdated rural woman
The alienated suburban woman
The overcrowded urban woman.

The woman who reads the news
The woman who has never made the news
The woman who starves herself to look right
The woman who starves.
The houseproud woman the tinker woman
The family woman the deserted woman

The woman who is colonised
The woman who is terrorised
The woman who is analysed
The woman who is advertised
The woman who is fertilised
The woman who is sterilised.

The woman who is locked in
The woman who is locked out
The woman in a prison cell
The woman in a convent cell
The woman who keeps her place
The woman who has no place.

The woman who loved her father too much
The woman who loved her mother too much
The woman who hates men
The woman who loves men
The woman who hates women
The woman who loves women.

The natural woman the perverted woman
The veiled woman the virgin woman
The celibate woman the prostitute woman
The jewish woman the buddhist moslem catholic
Hindu protestant woman
The french woman the irish woman

The chinese woman the indian woman
The african woman the american woman.
The upperclass upper middle class
Middle class lower middle class
Upper working class working class
Lower working class the no class woman.

The illegitimate woman the certified woman
The consumer woman the alien woman
The emigrant woman the immigrant woman
The decent woman the fallen woman
The mother of his children and
The other woman.

The articulate woman the illiterate woman
The bluestocking woman the ignorant woman
The deaf woman the blind woman
The loud woman the dumb woman
The big woman the petite woman
The flatchested woman

The look at those tits woman.
The ugly woman the femme fatale woman
The feminine woman the masculine woman
The painted woman the naked woman
The lilywhite and the scarlet woman.
The woman who thinks too much

The woman who never had time to think.
The woman who fights the system
The woman who married the system
The woman who swims against the tide
The woman who swells the tide that drowns
The woman who swims against it.

The woman who sends her sons to kill
The sons of other women.
The woman who sees her daughters
Murdered by the sons of other women.
The woman who is capitalised
The woman who is communised

The who ever heard of her woman
The who the hell is she woman
The who the hell does she think she is woman
The chaste woman the frigid woman
The vamp the tramp and the nymphomaniac woman
The wholesome woman the homely woman

The easy woman the tight assed woman
The ball breaking cock teasing
Doesn't know what she's made for woman.
The selfish woman the martyred woman
The sluttish woman the fussy woman
The loose woman the uptight woman

The naive woman the paranoid woman
The passive woman the dominant woman
The silly woman the hard woman
The placid woman the angry woman
The sober woman the drunken woman
The silent woman the screaming woman

Yes, that's it – thats the one
Why don't you write a poem for her –
The ordinary woman.

An ungrammatical poem.

And you,
the rain on our skin,
the sun beating,
you – sweet, guileful sister
of pleasure,
you said in my ear

my mind turning
my body in your hands
turning,
you said,
say my name
when you come

and I did
say it,
your name
say it as well
as I could,
coming so many times

which is perhaps why
rain beating, sun on the skin
I say it still sometimes,
your name, when I come
so long after
you went.

Gaining health by a gradual process of elimination.

Nothing much I can do –
unless you're prepared to give up –
ancient familiar words
of nuns, parents and priests.
The doctor pronounces them now
his little knife poised.

Nothing much I can do
unless you give up –
and I did,
everyone of them,
one by one,
stripped until my bones shone.

What else is left?
Sipping brandy,
wrapped in furs,
smiling my sister asks
– meat, men, cigarettes, booze,
anything else?

Oh yes,
one thing there was
and now its come round,
strange that it took them so long,
the one thing left unnoticed –
you.

Beginning.

She scoured and showered
her skin clear
dressed in fresh clothes
cut her hair and old friends
took up Aikido, celtic studies and zen
tore up snapshots and letters
painted all her wall white
smiled at each woman she passed in the street
and asked nobody home
who might find out
that for months she still slept
in your blood stained sheets.

Therapist.

What joy is there?
She asked me,with her cool,
unanswering therapist's eye,
quick to excuse,hesitation,half truth.
Any joy equal to the pain?
I could name none.
Not what you would title joy,
nothing large or unsullied
enough, for that.
I rifle my brain,

A quietness,or something like it,
could I offer in defence,
in crowded places,if our hands touch.
At railway stations,like an old movie
keeping pace with the carriage window,
breakfast on dark afternoons,
the smell of skin,
the line of bone
my mouth remembers better
than my eyes.

Walking six miles in rain
to finish an argument,
laughing sometimes,
making a plan.
Her eye waits, my own
downcast, in silence
I shuffle the file.
Not much to venture
against all this damage
I have brought for repair.

Songs of Peace

for a young woman marching against war
in the streets of Dublin

Women in the streets again,
hundreds in the streets again,
marching, holding hands,
singing frail songs against
death and destruction.
We don't want to die in your nuclear war.
At every barrier we stand and sing
into the visored eyes,
when they link arms against us we call
nuclear bombs kill gardai too.

We have turned full circle
to the sixties and hippies
scattering flowers for peace.
Nuns have joined us now,
changed their habits for tracksuits,
white masks on their faces
they carry black coffins
for sisters killed by soldiers.
We shall overcome, they sing.
Fifteen years ago I did not ask,

What or when or whom?
And you tell me with pride
you will stay all night in the park,
in the wet and the dirt and the dark,
laying your body down
between life and their weapons.
And yet you confide, with the
injured eyes of a child
refused, that when they arrested
you at the gate,

They shoved and taunted and abused.
And I have been told
that the women at Greenham wept
when they woke to find missiles
brought in while they slept,
as though patient protest
might establish a claim
to codes of war and fair warning.
And I wish you were right,
I wish it were true that

If women enough would gather,
women enough, would leave
husbands and children and sing,
laying their bodies down in the muck.
Yet how often before
have we offered our flesh,in hope,
in barter, in supplication?
And who will it please,if they come
for us, to find this time
we have made our own camps

Unarmed in the dirt and dark?
And I wish you were right
that songs and kisses could do,
hold back bullet and bomb,
loose power, reclaim the night.
But soldiers have always liked songs of peace,
and women have sung them to war before this,
and on return they have paid their respect,
have buried us bravely,buried us well,
with love and flowers and songs of peace.

J. P. HOLLERITH: I am white, middle-class, lesbian. Born in Canada, grew up there. Came to England to continue my academic research. Do almost anything but nowadays. Recently burst out of cast-iron closet via white-hot radical feminism; now keeping my head down while I sort out the hard bits. Participate in the local Lesbian Line. A few short stories of mine have been published in the U.K. and abroad in tiny science fiction/fantasy periodicals. I own a life-sized labyris and one of these days I am going to have the blades sharpened.

Annotations

We would have it otherwise
We on the margins
We slant-written against the text of the world
Scrawly and scribbly
We crowd round your black marks
Your rubricated headlines
We are your comment
We annotate, we say:
The text is not all there is, Not all
There is, not all.

IV

When two friends square off
Their voices are careful
Eyes down, lifted slowly, heavily.
And silences before speaking
Silences after speaking
Weighing the hurt, how much to reveal
How much not recognized till later
Remembering words;
Now aware of each others'
Hands, shoulders, heads
Turning, illuminated by lamplight
Each a pitying surgeon, probing straight down
The painful, clean blade of words
Cutting in, surprised at so much blood
It wells up over the scalpel completely.

Sleeping at my side

I look down at your exposed foot,
At a tuft of your hair up awry,
Your hand unfolding against the sheet,
And I ask myself what love is,
What my love for you is.
Is it when I stand with no barriers
Between your eyes and my true self?
Or when I do what is
Calculated to delight you — is this love?
Or the lust for approbation? How can I
Untangle safety
From the desire to live in your orbit?
Will I ever understand
What love is, when it's so freely given
And so easy to reclaim,
That it's almost an empty promise
Made to a stranger.

After The Day's Heat

If, after the day's heat
Finding three things,
A bird with brown fur wings
A plate with one line
No key in the door
Dissatisfaction chafes the
        Stretched evening;
Putting down half-read newspaper
                articles;
Washing not properly done;
Fret taken to its source
Am I going off her?

Post-call

It is stupid to give your heart
To someone who's going away.
You must fight that temptation
Every day.

Bereaving yourself foreknown
Is foolish as it's frail
Mere importunity
A jail.

You close the door behind you
And swallow the key:
That's love for you!
From me.

Connexion

Time is a train I've missed,
My hand nearly to the door;
It blurs past me in a streak of silver.
I'm left with a luggage of mine
Banging my knee, I look at the papers,
Butts, and cartons scattered under the rails,
The fretwork edge of the roof. So
Where do I go from here?

TINA KENDALL: A Black British woman of Jamaican origin. She grew up in Bradford, then moved to Manchester to study Modern Languages. She has been involved in a number of feminist projects, both in England and abroad and has lived in Germany, France and Australia while conducting research on feminist literary theory. She lives at present near Avignon with her young son and works at teaching, translating and writing.

expectations

i had thought that in aging
i would become one of those
high-cheeked
elegant
black women
composed
with assurance

. . . .

these days
i look in the mirror
often
it's dusty so the image
is deliberately hazy
(it's always the last thing
i clean)
what do i see
a face that's asking
questions and my cheeks
are yet to rise

tsmesis

in the V
     of her arm
a child (she is)
    but
what do we mean by
   modern what do we
mean by contemporary what
     do we mean by
     child

     a schism the wrong
word and the girl shakes
   the child this woman
    and loosens her arm
and there is surprise
   concern and no
cushion of wordlessness to
   capture it if
we move forward we forget
what (or subtle tones of
   what) we have left
     behind moved on be
hind contemporary modern
   a child

spring wind
for Annie

spring wind i
am in want of
the meadows
    the poppies
cornflowers
    come blow them to
me and in touching
    i'm tethered
      to trying to
        fly you

with me the sky
    slips the earth
turns the wheel burns
    my fingers are burning to(o)
      touching spring flowers
soft token of
trapped in the voice tones
    unheard yet of gentleness
drones the wind blowing
    spring flowers the sun shreds
the light warming down
    and my thoughts fly
my eyes shy
    my lips stick
i'm slipping and licking
    the love that's inside of

me came on so gentle
    so soft like the spots
of the rain drops the flowers
    bear witness to love in

spring wind

dawning I

ribbons of light slip into
the room morning dawns on two
strained bodies humped together
morning dawns of infinite potential
but too soon.

dawning II

her skin is night black
i touch it with care
her words are truth sharp

they spark in the air

we lie down together
we open our souls
we feel common feelings

we whisper our wishes
we share common goals

this love night ticks on
we're clasping caressing

this stillness is song

but then in slithers dawn
cast our magic away
she rises and walks out
for the break – of day

prolonging

"I will be free
no lover's kiss
to bind me to earth
no bliss of love
to counteract
actual bliss"
                    HD

she said passion prolongs
the minutes tick so long
un deux trois douze quinze
you put the phone down
ça va faire mal
passion prolongs she said
en tout cas c'est réciproque
when finally the phone call
came and you came
she clung on to the door
she needs a change – she thought
she'd never feel this way
her body aches her pores
are craving for your touch
and in the summer rain this
pool of passion spread
she drank wine to cool it
spent afternoons in bed to
stamp it out but just one glance

just one note of your voice just
the twist of your wrist just your
scent makes her eyes dim all
goes spinning flicker spinning
and to calm her think of eating
cherries together of marking the so
unreasonable distance she could
have rolled over made love
for hours and all this before
the passion was let loose [did
you know what you were doing
with the phone call] passion
prolongs and this is living
and the doubting fearing
dreaming wishing
kissing make it
bliss

SHEILA SHULMAN: Born in 1936, grew up in Brooklyn. My family were East European Jewish immigrants who struggled to stay alive. I have inherited most of their fears and some of their determination. I came to feminism late and reluctantly, having been sucker enough to think that humanism and left politics did include me. I unlearned a lot (the hard way), learned a lot, eventually (also the hard way). I'm still doing both. I could not have written anything had I not been for five years part of a women's writers group who encouraged, prodded, warmed me into beginning to find my own voice(s). I've lived in England since 1970 and am now studying to be a Rabbi – all the contradictions notwithstanding.

Square one   square one again
a bare desk   thin layer of dust
the typewriter sticks from disuse
outside through the dirty window
of a room   I can never call home
new leaves on an old tree
once   in the days when I read
War and Peace   each year
they might have seemed an omen
but   that was in another country
and I am hardly Prince Andrei

a few pages of notes
my distant past   Brooklyn
candy stores   the houses of my aunts
routes across the Bronx
a bowl of wax fruit
a samovar   a case of seltzer bottles

some more recent notes
dated ten years ago
rainbows and hot bread
raspberry brambles in Scotland
a tambourine tied to my pack
a weeping birch outside a room
in Primrose Hill   orange groves
in Israel   the pungent
Gallilean Hills

so much changed   all changed
since then
except this   my constant   infrequent
return
to square one

the lamp   the white mug of tea
the ashtray   old fag-ends
and how hard it is
just to sit here

Another drunk in the tube station tonight
his clothes were the same colour
as the floors
so I didn't see him coming
I was tired, thinking
I have to stop watching sometimes

he lurched toward me
raised his fist at me
spat into the air
he came on fast at a sharp diagonal
closed the distance between me and the wall
I ducked past him

I did think of knocking him off the platform
but kept walking fast toward the
WAY OUT sign
are they kidding?

drunks in the city
the odd, unlikely maniac
turning up in the friendly wood
or maybe just the local boys
out for a night on the town

I'm a woman on my own and glad of it
they don't like that so
I haven't felt safe in years
(except when I drove in a locked car
the year I had a car)

"Come on, lady
you sure you didn't ask for it?"

I've grazed your consciousness
struck your imagination
left no wounds yet
it's all harmless, interesting
you can still try to
fit me into your life

you've got a man, a house, a couple of kids
a lively populated life
and you're looking for a way
to find yourself

I'm a lesbian and a feminist
with not much use for men
talking to a few others of my kind
as we try to stay alive
in a world that doesn't yet exist
but is kicking to be born

these are all the necessary elements
for what Virginia Woolf called
metaphorically
(but we do not live in metaphors)
the drawn swords of an honorable antagonism

I'm not sure where to go from here
that depends partly on you
and whether you accept
the challenge in the air

because lady, if I should ever strike
more than your imagination
I won't be the only one
playing with fire

if you should once see
with your body
through my eyes
there'd be no going back
and lots of pain ahead

on the other hand
both of us playing with fire
on some high and windy hill
could make a glorious blaze

I'm only writing this because
I'm an arsonist at heart
and like you very much

also, out of old Platonic habit
I always carry kindling in my pocket

she and I were lovers
for awhile, a year ago

last night she slept in my bed again
(just passing through town)

the beginning of a child in her belly

I've never seen the man
it all happened someplace else

I hoped, as I tried to fall asleep
a careful distance away in the bed

that we might wake to find ourselves
in each other's arms again

she said, in the morning
that I looked sad

I shrugged as only a Jew can shrug
made tea, and left

This morning, though you aren't here
I kiss the bottom of your throat
just where the collar-bones meet
hold your naked breasts, lick and bite
bury my head between your legs
taste, and see
my tongue gently seeks your center
secret warm and salt

it is peace, it is play
even a couple of sleek brown otters
sliding down a mud-bank near
their stream in the woods
could not possibly be
so entirely at home
entirely themselves

I
the New Year
came and went
and the ten days
during which
in the sacred calendar
of my people
the whole creation
happens again each year
and each single soul
works to atone, to forgive
to be as new as the world

like my grandmother
I baked honeycakes
to sweeten the coming time
that was all I did

the Day of Atonement
came and went
I lit a candle
for a dead friend
for all my dead
that was all I did

for what shall I atone
and to whom
and who shall I presume
to forgive

II
some cakes, a candle
and soon a little spinning top
with a living letter
whose sacred meaning I do not know
on each of its four sides

fragments, gestures, a toy
still, again
I am half-embarrassed
distanced, slightly ironical
as usual

III
but at last
I am learning my language
the jargon, the joke
the speech of women

and from old, old stories
the fires of those
joy-drunk, god-drunk madmen
the Chassids
strike implausible sparks
in my lesbian, feminist heart

I speak again
though haltingly
in my own tongue
and read the crabbed print
my grandmother read
I hear the voices
of a murdered world

once again
I read story after story
this time, now, I cry
I recognize them
although
I do not exist in them
between us, the air is vexed
we need each other, but how?

tears have always been for me
a breaking open
I hold my ground
I do not turn my back
I have always secretly loved
the doctrine that talks about
the freeing of the holy sparks

For Colleen

drowned April 1980

I
well birdbones   we go back
a long way
an unlikely friendship
sealed ten years ago
in my shed of a kitchen

a red tile floor   old stove
corrugated plastic roof
wooden table   rickety chairs
bits of stained glass   in the windows
a door out to the rumpled garden
and lots of light

late summer
your lover had left you   suddenly
only a letter to say
she was back in the States
mine had left me already
more slowly

we hardly knew each other
you cried   I thought you needed to eat
tempted you with melon
I cried   all over the toast
you made small jokes
we peered at each other   out of bloodshot eyes
over our glasses   through the smoke
of too many cigarettes
eventually we laughed

II

years later   many changes later
we spent a perfect Christmas day
in a house suddenly quiet
after such storms
my lover's madness   my violence
a breather
you and I hated Christmas
it meant families
it meant   lovers going away
we ignored it   in style

in the warm house   in big jumpers
you sat in your room   I in mine
we read   wrote
met for tea   for scratch meals
in the evening   we sat around
smoked   talked

we liked each other
I think we even liked ourselves
we were easy together

III

later   I went to America
a mistake   but never mind
I had to go
to learn it wasn't home
after a year   I came back broken down
you meanwhile
(this is your language)
had crossed your freezing river
left behind   you said
the wolf shadow   your other self
the chronic suicide

I came back to find you
bright-faced   eager
your small body trembled
with the joy you said you'd found
I was glad for you
probably you couldn't tell
I only hoped it would last

faith in women   you said
sounds absurd   but it really was that simple
and all because you found a few
who shared your love of growing things
and a friend   new to you   but not to me
who acted as catalyst   populated your solitude
turned you inside out   made you feel
a sort of spiritual home
the possibility for all the words
we had never used   without inverted commas

she never knew   (I find this hard to understand)
how you were before
how desperate   how tired   how ironical
how half the time
you barely wanted   to stay alive
how the human world appalled you

all that time   I sat in a life's worth of rubble
you said to me   again and again
if I can do it   you can do it
you poured life into me
you were patient   you didn't give up
you stuck with me   talking   talking
it used to be me
who talked to you like that
fight   I'd said   fight
live   you said   live

IV

then the trouble came
as it inevitably would
(we do not live in our new world yet)
and it came from all directions
with your friends   with your lover
your spark of a common vision   soured
and you left needing
thrown back inside your head
spinning faster and faster
a desperate amateur of permutations

idiot   you spent that autumn
in a tent in a field
you   who had to have warmth   good food
no wonder you got pneumonia
and were left wasted
more than usually   down to bone
you didn't really mend
or so I told myself
to handle what came next

V

I'm going to Africa   you said one day
to see my country   my mother
if I don't come back   please understand
the ocean there is warm   I will have gone home
I'm tired   you said   I don't belong here
not on this earth   not anymore
don't tell anyone
I didn't

birdbones   birdbones
with eyes like yours
with hands like yours   on a camera
how could you want not to see
how could you leave what you saw
the rocks   the roots   the seaweed

I knew all the arguments
for wanting to go on living   on this earth
I used them all   as best I could
maybe they would have worked
if I'd believed them more
if I'd been more alive

that time   you did come back
but while I talked   and talked   and talked
you got thinner   and smaller   and lived
even more   only in your eyes

VI
then one day
there were   long strange letters   postmarked Penzance
I didn't even know you'd gone
we broke in   through an open window
found   files arranged considerately   a will for me
but your book burnt
the small flat neat   ineradicably yours
and o my god   the garden newly sown

I went to the Scilly Isles
you might have gone there
not to find you   but to say goodbye
in the place   that used to be called
the Blessed Isles   the Isles of the Dead

for form's sake   I asked
if anyone had seen you
old women   with kind blue eyes
wished me luck   gave me cups of tea

I looked for you
not for a body   but
for what you might have seen
that I had seen before   and loved
small gold shells   elephant rocks   tide pools
islands like dolphin backs   edged with spray
standing out   in the blue and friendly sea

if it had to be anywhere
I'm glad it was there

but birdbones   I wish I knew
was the water cold   and did your longing for peace
carry you   or was it hard
and where are you now
and what the hell am I supposed to do
without you

VII

but I am not quite without you   am I
I never imagined   I would feel like that

mourning you
I found our friend again
with whom   for years
I had barely been able to speak
we sat in your room
cried in turn   held each other
it was enough   a beginning

a while ago   I went to the Oxford Botannical Garden
where you had worked
I looked at the bog garden
I understood   at last
how and why you loved it best
the plants   the trees (I don't know names)
the stones   the tadpoles   flowers   newts and mud
one life   connected

I sat on a bench in the sun
looked at an ordinary tree
cried because it was there
and I could see it
I remembered you always called me   a fighter
I wanted to say   no Col no   not always
not only   not now

your gifts last
so they should
having cost you your life
rest   birdbones   rest
you live   one way or another
with us   in us

A Little Poem for Liz on What Is After All the First Day of Spring

my love you worry so
there has never been a year
without a spring
even I know that
I think when, perhaps, not whether

soon, we'll walk in a park
we'll see
laburnum, daffodils, forsythia
flaunting all at once
too much yellow, you'll say
your voice rebuking such
unthinking flamboyance
your eyes seeing the
contours, shadings, colours
of the garden
I know you'll make some day
in which such things cannot happen

but you thought spring wasn't going to happen at all
so there
and now you complain
you will look sheepish
I like to tease you
when I know it cannot hurt

you will say
there's too much yellow
and I will say
but where are the ducklings

this is a conversation
we have had each year
for some time now
two women, friends and lovers
walking quietly in a park
arm in arm

sometimes it is a relief
from our pain with each other
sometimes it is only me
looking, dimly, for "life"

but sometimes
to complain about the yellow
to be precipitate about the ducklings
is an effervescence
a luxury, a little heart-dance

because
while it is unlikely
that either of us will
become a bacchante
run drunk and wild with streaming hair
through Regent's Park
(two quiet women like us
with short hair
in the most English of English parks)

still, it is spring
we are together, still
the yellow will recede
for white and blue and all the young greens
the ducklings will turn up in time
and your hand on my face
will still be a miracle

I'll make no metaphors
about your naked flesh
it is itself, yours, you
comparable to nothing else
that is more than enough

each time we lie together
I am warmed by a soft
recurrent
shock

healed, safe
suddenly
from wherever I
am   alive again

MEG KELLY: was a journalist for more than 20 years and is now involved in adult education. She has a son and they live beside the sea and near the country.

The location is important, she says. "I'd feel stranded if I had to live away from the sea. I already feel a bit like old flotsam in the emotional 'wreckage' of feminism – committed intellectually to the tide of liberation, but still clinging to a tattered romanticism.

"My environment anchors me; I can always relate to it while the rest of my life is taking unexpected routes – it's the black and white in a world which, if human beings are to progress, must be many shades of grey."

Salt-sharp burnt skin
Sand clinging along the length of your
                        umber limbs
Slightly rasping beneath the whorls of
                        my fingers.
Lids of skin hide the infusion of love in
                        your eyes
Which, having swept me into their hot tide,
Now seal in that subterranean world of
                        incalescence
Where you swim.
And I beside you
Urge you down into those deeper sea-green
                        trenches
Where fantastic creatures
(Those coelacanths of the soul)
Glide and dive in voluptuous pleasure.
I moisten your eyelids
And am briefly permitted to flow with you
In the subaqueous currents of love.
I know where you are going –
Have I not just emerged
                        drenched
                        breathless
On the same shore.

Winter Beach

On a beach flowing away from under our feet
                        veils of sand in seaborne wind
Black threads of dead seaweed half-submerged
                        in ceaselessly shifting grit
                        varicose veins in the sand
Sea the colour of wet elephant skin
Rain as abrasive as pumice stone
                        freezing my forehead to the bone
                        scouring the thin flesh there.
Only my hands stay warm
                        knitted with yours
                        in my wet coat pocket.

Some Isolated Spot

Lozenges of shale
Like pink finger nails
In brackish pools rainbowed with oil.
Transparent seaweed (shreds of sloughed lizard skin)
Filming the greasy slick.
Mud asthmatically crackling
And curlews fluting beyond the grass islands.
Sea fret stealthily veiling the bay
Bringing the long-awaited squall
To spit against our skin,
Dripping through your hair (mercury beading copper
                              strands)
And onto your mouth that now presses mine
In a soft crush of rain-tasting lips.
I can feel your warm body
Through wet cloth.
There is in this gentle fusion a dismissal
Of fear and hurt.
Beneath the ambient sky (steaming marsh clay-coloured
                    under clouds of wet muslin)
Should anyone chance upon the viscous path above us
They will have to acquiesce
To the greater equation
Of lovers
Soaked in rain (and solitude).

New Dimension

With you there is always discovery . . .
Sometimes it is as if I have been sightless
Never having seen rooks spear the sky
Over leafless trees stalking icy ditches;
Wet flint shimmering through a winter window;
Sheep and redshank paddling in lonely meadows
Barbed with black damp spikes of hawthorn.
    And you
    Blue-boned with cold
    Against my soaked coat
My world acquires a new dimension
Beside a fire fed with dead elm
Spitting its fragments onto the tiles
While outside the cries of geese
And liquid bubbling of rain-filled streams.
    I always knew England was meant to be this
    But not who to share it with.

Better Your Scorn . . .

In a wilderness where owl-flight startles from
the secret mud
I, tormented, loved you
But did not touch
or say.
Through golden light trapped in black
timeless pools
We walked
And laughed
Afraid to touch
Or say.
In grey mud covered
And tired
We sat to share
A skin-tight silence
Dying to touch
Or say.
Birds glided up-river
Shoo-ed by the wind
And the dogs whined like keeners
Worried that we might never move again.
Their whimpering echoed my despair
On that cloying shore.
Birds angered by our intrusion
Seemed to scream
SAY SAY SAY
Until I could no longer bear not to –
Better your scorn than never knowing.

Blizzard

Courting the storm's menace
Eyes squinting against its sting,
We do not envy the women who stayed inside
Sheltered from this delicious dangerous
swirling world
by double-glazed minds
and senses deadened
in ankle-deep Axminster
never perhaps dreaming
as we crunch past in the soft exhausting fall-out
of rough wet bark against the spine
of eyes that mirror the sea's kaleidescopic moods
of that fox-quick smile.
We welcome the sinister twisting pillars
spiralling across the sullen waves
dark blizzards draped between them.
Soon that blinding curtain will envelop us
And we shall taste it
Even as my mouth tastes yours
Crushing the flakes of snow clinging
to your skin
tonguing the warm moisture
from your lips.
We do not hide from the demonic storm
we hide in it
Dreading its inevitable exhaustion.

RUTH ADAM: Born in Dublin 1946. I went to school & University there and left in 1967 to go to Vancouver via New York. I loved New York and vowed to return within 2 years but ended up living in the middle of the Canadian Rockies and working as a cow-girl for a time. This was a searing business which produced only a handful of poems years later when the horror had worn off.

I then wanted to live in Paris for a couple of years and would never have left it had it not been for my inability to break the language barrier. So arrived in London in 1971; this coincided nicely with the rise of Gay Liberation and made coming-out a reality. I now live in a North London suburb which according to a national newspaper is full of people like myself ie. a middle-aged media person embarking on a second relationship. I have 2.4 cats.

Horses live so long.

Friend, we're bored.
                    We who worried
about the language barrier
lived these long months saying nothing
in what is more or less our own language.
Now I hate you for the way
you walk across a room.
Horses live so long, the saying goes,

because they never try and analyse
their relationships.   I try to think
more of an environment,
perhaps a field . . . .
flat and brown as a penny.

but only one thought acrobats in my head.
I've heard that nothing we say dies
it travels on and on
mumbling itself out into space.

for Cathy Nicholson

Engrossed in motherhood, one friend
wiped the various orificial slimes.
Another in her way
painted girls as langourous food

arranging them in a pale and startling salad.
Some friends managed both.
More power to them, thought Mary-mary,
she hankered after slavery not dedication,

disliking herself for it.   Had eye
and eye been hearts this weather
they'd have never opened, in these doldrums
things done with conviction impressed her.

All year she dissipated herself
in usefullness.   Had things taken
a different turn
she'd have been good to come home to.

The Camp-fire and the Dark.

It is dark now and in the wood behind us
pheasants drag their tuneless rattles
suggesting something more dire
than headlands in east anglia.
They are curious, I suppose, at such
a large fire in this part. "I dont like it there"
my child says, embracing the whole wood
with one small arm. "Can pheasants harm us?"
No, I say, all creatures are afraid
of fire and we are the firemakers.   Besides,

we eat them. She sleeps at last,
wrapped in coats.   Her brother tends the fire
wearing a man's hat he found on the beach.

The sea shines but is silent.   The flames
reflect on their faces
and four incongruous roses bloom in the dark wood.

Arles, September 1977.

I

In a blue limb of the Rhône
the white-boned carcass of an old bridge
collapses.   Now that it has
almost reached the sea, the river
is relentless.   Broken fences abound
from here to the Mediterranean.

II

The shutters flatten
on closed hotels, dark flowers
have gone from the window-sills.   The fountain
drops confidently now, not one child
or noise disturbing its line.   The night
shades in this town,
a kindness of yellow lights surrounding
the dark eye of the square:
after years, it all accuses, time has not
changed the heart into a brave thing.

Lumber room.

She was her own chinese box.
Rooms revisited used the trick
of making themselves exactly smaller.
They had nothing to do
with the long afternoon of a life,
the long line with bright knots.
The selfish centre only mourns
for itself, thin part of the head
sitting up there to watch
the body rut itself into memory.

At the finish of all this it was
not her face the world saw, she became
graceful with her imagination.
That year she limped, learning
to love the sound of her own footsteps.

Trying to travel.

Awe-struck with the metropolis heart
I watch the endless boats, clumsy but noiseless.
Their stealth on the river.
Their know-how!
A whistle sends some gulls
complaining for awhile. Fearlessly they settle

on the station roof,
though it rises like a dragon's back,
studded and sleepy,
hulking its portion of the sky.
I can see it in the snow . . . .
its only frivolity.

The day so far, travelled
differently from others.
It may be I'm a crank,
refusing to close the windows
even for sleep. But echoes eventually
travel back with messages, whirling the gulls
this far inland.

GILLIAN HANSCOMBE was born in Melbourne, Australia in 1945. She has lived in England since 1965. She has one child, Martin Hanscombe. Her books include: *Hecate's Charms*, Sydney, 1976; *Between Friends*, Boston, 1982 and London, 1983; *Rocking the Cradle – Lesbian Mothers* with Jackie Forster, London, 1981, and 1982, Boston, 1982; *The Art of Life – Dorothy Richardson and the development of feminist consciousness*, London and Ohio, 1982; *Title Fight* with Andrew Lumsden, London, 1983.

SUNITI NAMJOSHI was born in Bombay, India in 1941. She has worked as an officer in the Indian Administrative Service. Her books include, among others: *The Jackass and the Lady*, Writers Workshop, India, 1980; *The Authentic Lie*, 1982 and *From the Bedside Book of Nightmares*, 1984, Fiddlehead Poetry Books, Canada; *Feminist Fables*, Sheba Feminist Publishers, London, 1981; *The Conversations of Cow*, The Women's Press, London, 1985. She teaches English Literature at Scarborough College, University of Toronto.

Narrative distance

Climb up here on this readymade mountain,
sit beside me, and watch the two women
walking on the beach, observe their relation,
mood and emotion, each connected to each.
One of them laughs, the other smiles; they appear
uninhibited, careless, carefree;
but our function is to watch – that is quite clear –
from our position of vantage we can see
into things. They are digging in the sand,
then they stop, consult one another, then proceed.
And now they are walking hand in hand;
they are picking up pebbles, sea-shells, sea-weed.
I feel they are deeply absorbed in making
something. I glance at your face. Would you agree?
What a lot of notes you seem to be taking.
I look back again, and to my dismay
the two of them have gone – just walked away.
Suddenly I'm reckless, "Let's go and see."
We scramble down the slope, but there's nobody
there, just the two of us, anxious, unready . . .

Reply to your poem of the same . . .

Yes they walked and watched and
wound arms when they weren't thinking about it and
wavered when they did. And yes the
two they watched
disappeared without permission.

What to make of it? Did
the oily sun have relevance or not?
And must the watchers quarrel about
who started it all and why?

The teaching says it is good to be puzzled;
it postpones confidence and inflates decisions;
and anyway, the watchers – being poets –
know each other's weakness, that they
observe only themselves (as is the
custom of their profession).

But we may, nonetheless, return to the narrative.

The women are unable to disappear. They must be
tumbling under the sleek surf,
tumbling between the dunes. Must
kiss lightly, touch briefly, gather shells.
At this distance, they must feel no pain.

We have dismissed them, says one watcher,
    suddenly troubled,
with a lie.
No, says the other; as a lie.

Perhaps, said the first, gravely, it's the sun after all;
it can drain away the colours.
And they can't have gone, says the other,
peering out to sea.

Explanation

I
No Daffodil

Why do you write about plants and animals?
                        Why not people?

Because
        no daffodil shrieks to be plucked,
                no lily rages, "Admire my bower."
        And if dogs go about and shit
                their shit, at least it mixes
                                with the stones and mud.
Somebody screeches that the trees
        have scattered their leaves in her garden.
O untidy trees, O vexing dogs,
        but they do not enter the house to be fed,
        they make no work, to which she says,
        "That is not true." And, of course,
        there is a sense in which it is not.
But if ordinary people would behave like trees,
        or like cats and dogs, or better still
        like the wilder animals, then I could admit
        a dispassionate liking for each one of them,
        the ugly and ignoble, the squat and the tall.
Someone explains,
        "A tree is not a person. A boy is not a cat."
"Yes," I reply, striving for patience,
        "That is the problem. Precisely that."

II
A Difference

But surely, she says, there are some
            you love, some you trust?
Me, for example. Think of me
        please as some sort of flower.
It's easy enough. We're sitting
                    on the grass.
She looks exactly
            like a gigantic flower.
So I say to her,
            but she still looks sad.
"There is a difference,"
            she tells me gently,
"between a simile
            and a genuine metaphor."

Corollary to Explanation

Sometimes seeing is l/ike
daffodils or lilac
                    (first you see them then you don't)
accepting the bleak of weather
                    (stems bald or just beheaded)
as if a single flame, a singular flower
can justify the rooting underground
(in atonement for light);

and the creatures (sound
echoing sense,
                    booming and blooming both) p/resent
(is it?) an unequal match,
                    indifferent by natural virtue,
to changing a point of view. (It's the shift of tone,
the tense of touch, gives such emphasis
to flowers, beasts

unlikely landscapes; seen
is not seeing.)
                    (If they could choose, they'd rather
                                        be used
than be eaten, rather be metaphors)
                    and any gigantic flower
is, after all, a need in the eye of the beholder.
Sometimes seeing is like daffodils or lilac
in atonement for light.

Hecate's Charm 4

Hecate said

what is there
apart from
I think of you
and
I dare not say

I cannot bear you to falter
that is my weakness

I can only address you
by names you will accept

I want to drink tea with you
talk about painting

I am not so moved by
your moving:
it is a nervous habit
brought on by being near me

we need to be
just out of touch

when we are close
one of us is always afraid

my trouble is
to reject your nobility
and
to admire your weakness

your trouble is that
I love you

Hecate's Charm 8

Hecate asked me,
when you are waiting for a lover to come
do you adorn yourself
or do you lie panting
or do you sit composedly reading Wittgenstein
or do you walk around with a domestic air
or do you idle with a poem?

I said
it depends on the kind of lover.

Maternity

I feel you stir, my nameless, like
leaves in their first dawnwakening wind;
featherfaint, you feel, then still.
Subtle and continual you are.

You did not ask to have me host
and yet you share my elements;
the moods of wind in summer leaves
my flesh translates for both of us.

I feel you stir as if you know
already how we shall unjoin;
you to your own summers given,
me to my separate self returned.

An Intentionalist Fallacy

There she sits saying that lyrics are antique
but without the robust charm of furniture. Why
not an article, a story, why not (even better) a
piece with political relevance? It's not that she
doesn't know how to read, either. Then she says
why not act rather than write?

There he sits saying love is a sickness and he's
happy to be free of it. And why put old wine etc.?

Then there's the wind outside my house. That's
all right, I think, since physics teaches the
randomness of the universe and mystics teach
detachment. (He says literature teaches nothing,
being unable to solve problems.)

He's easier gone. But she (her mouth to mine, her
breasts)?? (My journey?)

And whether I word her now, or not: is that an act?

Plotting

The distance to strive for, being
psychogeometric, is the
longest line between two points.

Detachment reached by this route can,
nevertheless, prove a mere diversion.

Ethics

Bombs, axes, all
objectifications of
meditated destruction I

refuse by act of grace to
subdue or be subdued by,

thinking myself thus fit.

Instead I hold
helpless in my
fierce arms my
last imputed cause,

my lover,
my betrayer.

An Apostrophe to Her Majesty
Queen Elizabeth II

You may have this book, if you like, though from
all I've been told, I can't imagine you'd like it;
there are words that may not be used in addressing you,
words that signify the unseemly,
female words.

                So all I can say is, take this book.
There are others of my kind in your kingdom.
And we feel not-smiled upon.

                    Your
grandfather's grandmother, we're told, didn't
believe in us. But
just like anyone we
lick your head into shape on the corners of our letters,
trade with your image among one another.

                              Like
anyone, we can see you move on immaculate horses
by courtesy of cameras.

                It's
even likely, given our knowledge, that
some of us share your bloodline.
So take this book; it implies no dishonour;
and queens have been known to dissent from the fathers.

The Return Of The Giantess

There were the usual reverberations,
                              a racket
in the sky, birds squabbling
                    and swerving and mating,
fanfare of flowers, feathers
                              falling,
that sort of thing.
                         There were
the subterranean tremors,
                    the ambiguous weather,
hot and cold spells,
              and the unambiguous dreams.
That the return of the giantess
                    would be noiseless
and reticent was not to be expected.
                    I had had warning.
But when she came, bending the green wave
of grass before her, treading the mountains
and – though courteous as ever – trampling
                              the hills,
and I opened my arms wide,
                         and wider
to receive her, neither grass, nor sky,
nor the pounding sea could hold her in,
and I held her close and we had our fill.

The Lion Skin

I

That in some dream I might be a lion
walking nobly and happily through a wood,
and that some lady, who has had her eye on
me, might say to me I am both great and good.
And then in this dream may this lovely lady
ruffle my yellow mane and trim my claws
and lead me to a spot green and shady,
but here the dream fails. I'm forced to pause.
For what do we say, this lady and I?
What happens next? Do I remove my skin?
And what does she do? Is she shocked and shy?
Or civil, and removes her own clothing?
I've never had the courage to dream the dream through,
but I think she says, "You be me, and I'll be you."

II

"Delectable, firm and juicy, such fair flesh
is good to eat." It was not I who said that,
it was the lady, and I, caught in the mesh
of light and leaves, could only lie there, and let what
might befall, quickly befall me. She took
such pleasure in each simple incision
that unwilling to betray by a word or look
I felt anything, I admired her precision
as slowly she flayed me. But there's a pleasure
in the nerve ends that makes one want to scream.
At last I screamed. And such was the measure
of this rare lady and such her supreme
and unexampled skill that she made me scream
again and again and long to wake and still to dream.

III

Dispense with disguises. The lion's skin
is a skin after all. Spread it on the ground,
so that no twig or stone in this forest clearing
shall hurt or trouble us when we both lie down.
Or should the weather change and we grow cold,
let the fur cover us and warm our sleep
till we wake again and are brave and bold.
And if the stars choose to peep, let them peep.
What can stars or moon or sun discover?
That the lady is a woman, and I,
who lie so close beside her, am her lover?
The stars will not shriek, will make no outcry.
The stars are sensible, and would not sever
woman from woman or lover from lover.

IV

I'd been dreaming again and in the dream
everything was lovely. You were very kind.
We'd finished making love and I felt serene.
When suddenly your voice: "Do you mind
not making love without permission;
I am not the creature of your fantasy."
I squirmed, I did not know which way to turn
because you were real, at least, real to me.
And so I lied. I said, "I do not know
who you are. For though you look like her, she
is kind, and her voice gentle, soft and low.
Oh you could not be whom you seem to be."
You answered, "No, I am not what I seem."
With that you vanished and I clutched my dream.

V

And yet there's a poetry of penury
that far outdoes the paeans of plenitude,
and the gorgeous dream blooms without injury
only in the hermit's austere solitude.
By which I mean that sometimes my arms ache,
my nostrils twitch, and I feel, or almost feel,
your body's warmth, and then sometimes I fake
the rest, cast caution aside, and make a meal
that would make an emperor look askance.
That I crave, desire and solicit you
is known to us both, and that I may not advance.
And since there is nothing I can say or do,
I tell myself that the dream is made of such stuff
that to dream is best and the dream enough.

VI

The thick, tough skin of the lion shall be chopped
and snipped to make six balls, which, when filled with air,
shall go spinning crazily like the lopped
heads of poets crammed with passion and despair.
And you, while walking through the woods some day,
might chance to glance at these leathern orbs
and seize them and make much mirth and holiday.
I shall be content, for the dream that absorbs
me can have no other end. Thus held and seen
it is real, and still real, again and again,
whenever you choose. And what might have been
is cause for contemplation, banishes pain.
Then all shall be well, and by the grace of the muse
this lion skin shall still give pleasure and prove of use.

Triptych

I

A PLACID COW was grazing in the meadows. She wasn't really thinking about anything, except perhaps about the texture of the grass, its springy resilience, about a patch of clover, about the taste of buttercups, about flies, and the warmth of the sun beating on her back. In other words she was simply grazing. When suddenly a half-grown lion cub bounded from the woods. It was a ball of sunshine, a bundle of joy. It danced up to the cow and licked her all over with its rough tongue. It was importunate. It was friendly. It insisted that the cow play with it. And the cow, poor beast, was so exceedingly flattered, she soon complied, to the end that you see: a penitent cow, and an astounded lion cub begging piteously for a piece of beef.

The point of the tale? It depends rather on which of the two you identify with.

II

AND YET the cow we are speaking of was a Brahmini cow, had the long slender legs of Indian cattle, the quiet eyes, wistful and expressive, the curving horns, the elegant dewlap, and that masterly sweep from shoulder to rump which seems to say this is the way cattle should be made, this and only this. And she was skinny – all the better to admire her bones, their indisputable integrity. What is more, though not tended and praised as a goddess ought to be, she was used to some lip-service. This she accepted gently and calmly, never once altering her docile expression; and when chased out of gardens with sticks and stones, it is true that she ran, but she ran with a slow and clumsy dignity. So much for this beast. And what of the cub? The golden lion cub whose genes proclaimed a royal heredity? They played together these incongruous two, the burnished cub against her white flanks making them look like a scene from heraldry. Oh they were beautiful. They were gleaming. They recalled the world before the fall. They were like milk and honey.

III

CONVERSELY Moon-Calf in love with the Lady Lioness: "O Queen of the Jungle, Princess of Night, allow me, if you will, to entertain you with my grief." Lioness a little anxious, has other things to do, but Moon-Calf distracting and rather dazzling in the light of moonbeams. Speaks to the Moon-Calf: "Go away, Moon-Calf. Come back in another five years. Then we shall see." Five years elapse. Moon-Cow returns. Lioness and Moon-Cow become excellent friends, lovers as well, pick pretty patterns in the smooth moonbeams.

Crow and Starling

Once upon a time there was an idiot crow. She was sensible enough most of the time, but utterly foolish when she fell in love or fancied anybody. Now, it so happened that she met a starling. The starling was charming, the crow was charmed, but she decided that for once she was going to be sensible. She was calm, dispassionate and moderately friendly. At last one day they met again. Crow had pined and repined dreadfully, but in accordance with her decision to do nothing foolish, she had done nothing. Once again Starling and Crow were very sensible and reasonably friendly. Soon they began to meet often. They continued calm, quiet and friendly. It became a habit. They got used to it. So that it was only occasionally that Crow tore her feathers and cursed her wisdom and her folly.

Ordinary Women

I had got it all wrong –
                              about who
was supposed to rescue whom,
                              who was to judge,
who to watch, and which one of us
        was expected to set the world aright.
'Puzzling,' I thought. I looked
              at the leaves, the trees.
I imagined the creatures hidden
                          in the leaves.
I would rather be a plant.
                      But those who were tall
we turned into knights. Those who were womanly –
                      that was obvious enough.
And those who were kingly we made
              into kings; though the armour
didn't fit, and some women said
        they didn't know what a lady was.
"But that's okay," everybody said.
                      "We'll re-design, re-adjust."
I was a knight –
        I was courteous, I was tough, but not
              tall enough. I sat among the women
                          and watched the knights.
I lounged among the knights and watched
                          the women. At last
somebody said, "This really won't do."

So we all got up.
We mixed and we mingled, we shared
                    a common cause.
Halfway through it all I fell in love.
    "There is no wooer and no one is wooed,"
            my lady informed me.
"Fine," I replied and looked expectant.
            "And you are not a knight."
"No," I agreed. She nodded approval.
            "And what this means
is that you and I are equals in love."
        "Yes," I said smiling happily,
"we love one another like two ordinary women."
            But she quickly demurred,
"I was always a lady — "
            And at last I understood.
"Right," I said. "You are a lady, and I
            am a lesbian.

A Consummation . . .

They said that all the armourers have gone, that the men got discouraged, died out, gave up. They said that all the costumers have faded, their ideas have faded, their craft. The barbaric women have taken over. They dance naked. Their breasts joggle. Their hair is uncut. Pallid patriarchs turn away nervously. Their shadowy faces twist with disgust. By an act of the will they achieve annihilation. Their ghosts give up the earth. But the beautiful barbarians partner each other. They lie down on the grass, they make love.